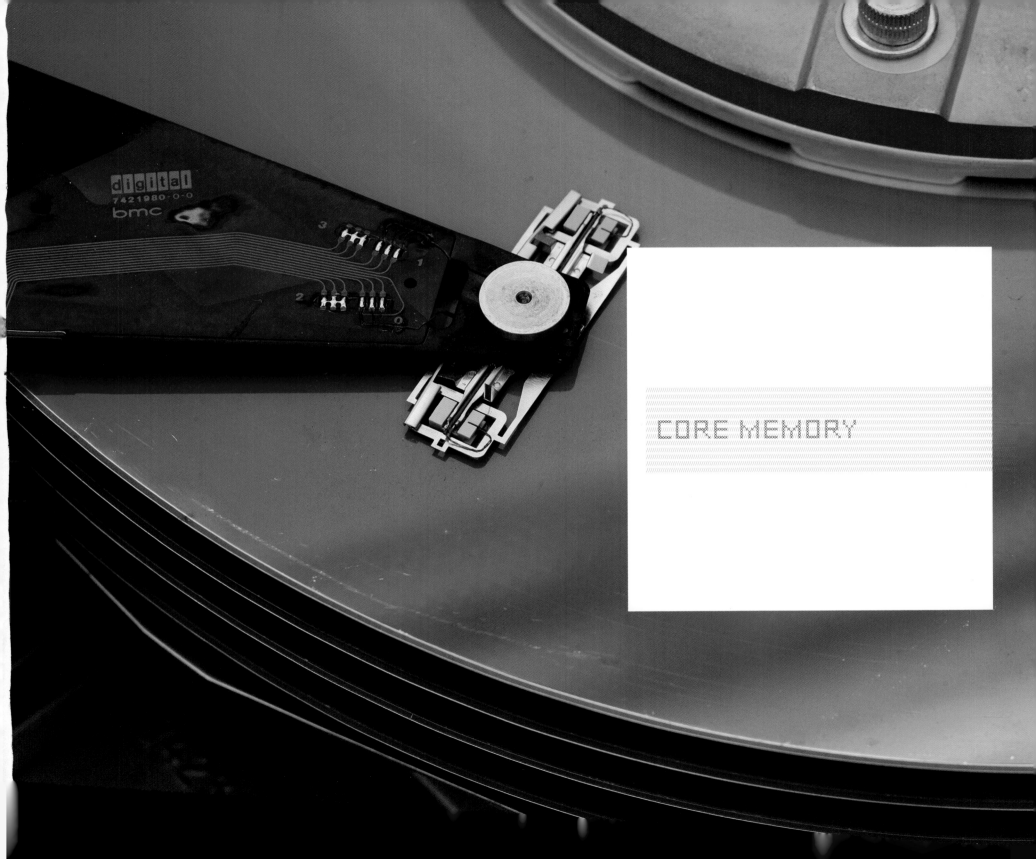

CORE MEMORY

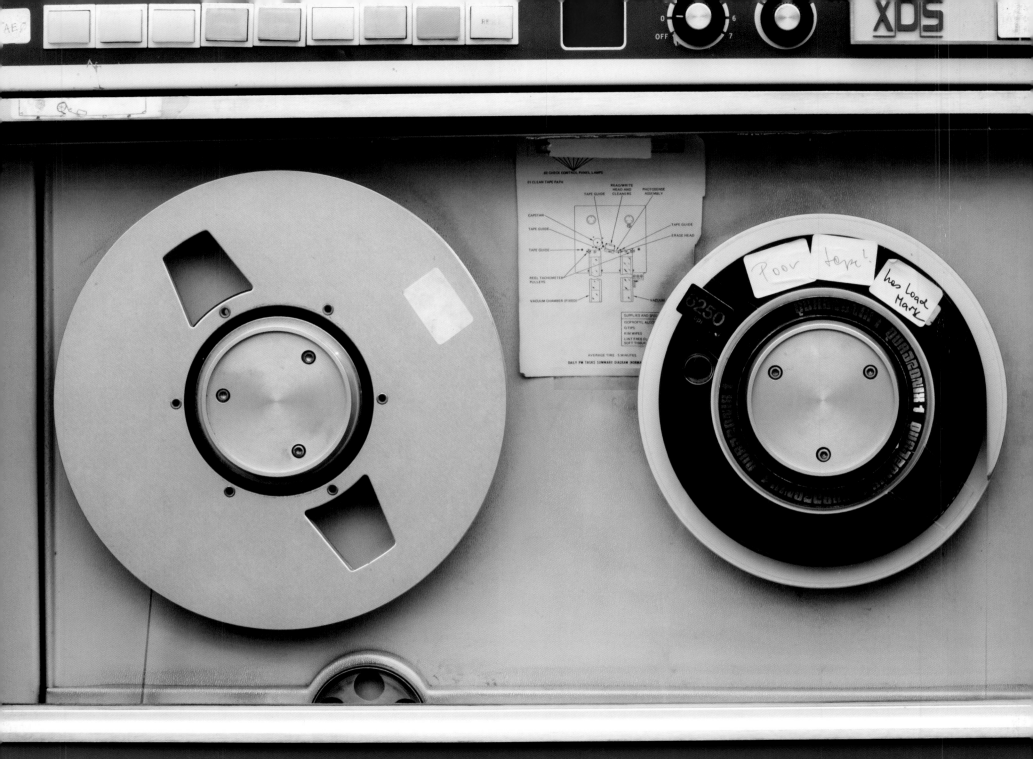

CORE MEMORY

A VISUAL SURVEY OF VINTAGE COMPUTERS
FEATURING MACHINES FROM THE COMPUTER HISTORY MUSEUM

PHOTOGRAPHS BY MARK RICHARDS   /   TEXT BY JOHN ALDERMAN   /   FOREWORD BY DAG SPICER

CHRONICLE BOOKS
SAN FRANCISCO

LIBRARY OF CONGRESS CATALOGING-IN-PUBLICATION DATA AVAILABLE.

ISBN-10: 0-8118-5442-6

ISBN-13: 978-0-8118-5442-9

MANUFACTURED IN CHINA.

BOOK DESIGN BY PRIMARY&CO. / WARREN CORBITT

10 9 8 7 6 5 4 3

CHRONICLE BOOKS LLC

680 SECOND STREET

SAN FRANCISCO, CALIFORNIA 94107

WWW.CHRONICLEBOOKS.COM

P.1: DEC HARD DRIVE ASSEMBLY, 1970
P.2: SIGMA-5 MAINFRAME, 1967
P.4: APOLLO GUIDANCE COMPUTER, 1968
P.5: IBM MODEL 077 COLLATOR, 1937
P. 6-7: IBM MODEL 077 COLLATOR PUNCH CARD, CA. 1970

1	2	3	4	5	6	7	8	9	10	11	12	13	14	15	16	17	18	19	20	21	22	23	24	25	26	27	28	29	30	31	32	33	34	35	36	37	38	39	40	41	42	43	44	45	46	47	48	49	50	51	52

0 0 0 0 0 0 0 0 0 0 0 0 0 0 0 0 0 0 0 0 0 0 0 0 0 0 0 0 0 0 0 0 0 0 0 0 0 0 0 0 0 0 0 0 0 0 0 0 0 0 0 0

1 2 3 4 5 6 7 8 9 10 11 12 13 14 15 16 17 18 19 20 21 22 23 24 25 26 27 28 29 30 31 32 33 34 35 36 37 38 39 40 41 42 43 44 45 46 47 48 49 50 51 52

1 1 1 1 1 1 1 1 1 1 1 1 1 1 1 1 1 1 1 1 1 1 1 1 1 1 1 1 1 1 1 1 1 1 1 1 1 1 1 1 1 1 1 1

2 2 2 2 2 2 2 2 2 2 2 2 2 2 2 2 2 2 2 2 2 2 2 2 2 2 2 2 2 2 2 2 2 2 2 2 2 2 2 2 2 2 2 2 2 2 2 2 2 2 2 2

1 2 3 4 5 6 7 8 9 10 11 12 13 14 15 16 17 18 19 20 21 22 23 24 25 26 27 28 29 30 31 32 33 34 35 36 37 38 39 40 41 42 43 44 45 46 47 48 49 50 51 52

3 3 3 3 3 3 3 3 3 3 3 3 3 3 3 3 3 3 3 3 3 3 3 3 3 3 3 3 3 3 3 3 3 3 3 3 3 3 3 3 3 3 3 3 3 3 3 3 3 3 3

4 4 4 4 4 4 4 4 4 4 4 4 4 4 4 4

1 2 3 4 5 6 7 8 9 10 11 12 13 14 15 16 17 18 19 20 21 22 23 24 25 26 27 28 29 30 31 32 33 34 35 36 37 38 39 40 41 42 43 44 45 46 47 48 49 50 51 52

5 5 5 5 5 5 5 5 5 5 5 5 5 5 5 5 5 5 5 5 5 5 5 5 5 5 5 5 5 5 5 5 5 5 5 5 5 5 5 5 5 5 5 5 5 5 5 5 5 5 5 5

6 6 6 6 6 6 6 6 6 6 6 6 6 6 6 6 6 6 6 6 6 6 6 6 6 6 6 6 6 6 6 6 6 6 6 6 6 6 6 6 6 6 6 6 6 6 6 6 6 6 6 6

1 2 3 4 5 6 7 8 9 10 11 12 13 14 15 16 17 18 19 20 21 22 23 24 25 26 27 28 29 30 31 32 33 34 35 36 37 38 39 40 41 42 43 44 45 46 47 48 49 50 51 52

7 7 7 7 7 7 7 7 7 7 7 7 7 7 7 7 7 7 7 7 7 7 7 7 7 7 7 7 7 7 7 7 7 7 7 7 7 7 7 7 7 7 7 7 7 7 7 7 7 7 7

8 8 8 8 8 8 8 8 8 8 8 8 8 8 8 8 8 8 8 8 8 8 8 8 8 8 8 8 8 8 8 8 8 8 8 8 8 8 8 8 8 8 8 8 8 8 8 8 8 8 8 8

1 2 3 4 5 6 7 8 9 10 11 12 13 14 15 16 17 18 19 20 21 22 23 24 25 26 27 28 29 30 31 32 33 34 35 36 37 38 39 40 41 42 43 44 45 46 47 48 49 50 51 52

9 9 9 9 9 9 9 9 9 9 9 9 9 9 9 9 9 9 9 9 9 9 9 9 9 9 9 9 9 9 9 9 9 9 9 9 9 9 9 9 9 9 9 9 9 9 9 9 9 9 9 9

TABLE OF CONTENTS

FOREWORD

AUTHOR   DAG SPICER

..//

What computers mean to us depends largely on what we bring to them. Our expectations, our past experience, the dreams and myths that surround them, their physical characteristics–all these aspects resonate on multiple, often overlapping levels.

One level is aesthetic. Many nonspecialists in the computer arts enjoy these machines for their visual appeal and curiosity. Nearly everyone, regardless of technical background, can appreciate the intricacies of a computer's mechanical design, its rows of switches and blinking lights, its often ungainly proportions, and the personal connection they feel when they recognize the first computer they used.

A second level is important for specialists. People trained in computer science or electrical engineering bring the additional dimension of how these objects illuminate abstract principles of computer architecture and the ideas immanent in their design–ideas that give us insight into the minds of their designers and the challenges they faced.

A third level is the historical trajectory of these objects: how they were financed and why, what problems they were trying to solve, and the mistakes made and dead ends encountered by their designers. We learn a lot by understanding these human elements and how they shaped historical and technical factors into stable artifacts, in turn stitching together the fabric of today's information-based society.

Each of these three levels can be applied to all artifacts of human culture, from the earliest bone tools of *Australopithecus* more than two million years ago to the most advanced modern operating systems of today. With time, items with complex overlapping levels of interpretation like these can eventually collapse into hermetic objects, or "black boxes." For this reason, curators and museums, through their exhibitions and programs, are necessary. Without them, there isn't direct communication with the viewer, no mechanism for teasing out these levels. Without them, there is no longer an understanding of *how* something was developed–only the object itself, uninterpreted, or, conversely, only secondary sources and no object, like Hamlet without the Prince.

The Computer History Museum is home to the world's largest collection of computer artifacts and serves as a way station for us to catch our collective breath by opening these black boxes. It does this by paying attention to the three interpretive levels described above. The museum carefully preserves the artifacts themselves (aesthetic); explains their technologies and context (technological); and relates how they came into and, ultimately, out of being (historical).

>

FOREWORD

AUTHOR   DAG SPICER

..//

Mark Richards's wonderful photographs capture the fascinating machines in the museum's collection from a hyper-aesthetic viewpoint, while John Alderman's text speaks to their unique historical context. The period covered in this book spans from the first giant machines–such as the room-filling ENIAC–to very recent personal computers.

Today, the compaction of transistors into ever smaller spaces has made available to almost anyone the computer power that formerly was the preserve of well-funded institutions. This has, in turn, transformed computers from number crunchers into generic platforms for visualization, entertainment, and communication, mediating almost all of our interactions with the modern world. Billions of computations and logical operations still take place every second inside the black box, but the fraction of computers used as supercalculators gets smaller with every Tivo, iPod, cellular phone, and car sold. It is *information*, not only mathematical results, that is produced, exchanged, and transformed, becoming the very lifeblood of the twenty-first century as oil was in the twentieth and steam was in the nineteenth.

How do we make sense of all this?

With historians still debating the impact of the French Revolution more than two hundred years ago, it seems unlikely that we shall be able to digest fully the impact of the computer–barely fifty years old–for a long time to come. We are simply too embedded in its history, and it in us–from the moment we are born to our last breath. But we should still try. Reflecting on computers as visual milestones, as this book enables us to do, allows us to step back and appreciate them in a different context, one with a deep and rich history, rather than as objects isolated in time with no connection to what has gone before them.

Computers, like all artifacts, are made by people and reflect their strengths and weaknesses, their brilliance and their follies. I hope that as you enjoy this book, and the unique interpretive lens of Mark Richards and the essays by John Alderman, you will discover computers as objects of beauty that also mirror the human condition in all its richness, struggle, and creativity.

DAG SPICER
SENIOR CURATOR
COMPUTER HISTORY MUSEUM, MOUNTAIN VIEW, CALIFORNIA

NAME	**Z3 ADDER** (RECONSTRUCTION)
YEAR CREATED	**1941** (RECONSTRUCTED 1999)
CREATOR	RAUL ROJAS/KONRAD ZUSE
MEMORY	64 WORDS

..//

In the midst of World War II, the world's first programmable, automatic electromagnetic computer was built by a German, civil engineer Konrad Zuse. Surprisingly, though it was presented to fellow German scientists, not much was made of it at the time, and it was destroyed in 1944 during an Allied bombing raid on Berlin. This is a re-imagining (for teaching purposes) of the adder unit of that destroyed machine, which used twenty-four hundred telephone relays as switches for memory, instead of vacuum tubes, and hole-punched movie film as a storage medium.

Zuse had been called up for military service but convinced the recruiters that he was better used creating computers, and one of his machines was used to produce glide bombs. Despite that brush with the army, Zuse received very little war funding, and his work was not widely known. Some speculate that the Z3 would have been much more significant without the war—especially since the Allied competition was driven so heavily by military investment.

After the war, in 1946, IBM optioned Zuse's patents. Zuse used that money to start his own computer company, the Zuse-Ingenieurbüro Hopferau (changed to Zuse KG in 1949), which successfully built many other computers and was finally bought by Siemens in 1967.

GESPERRT

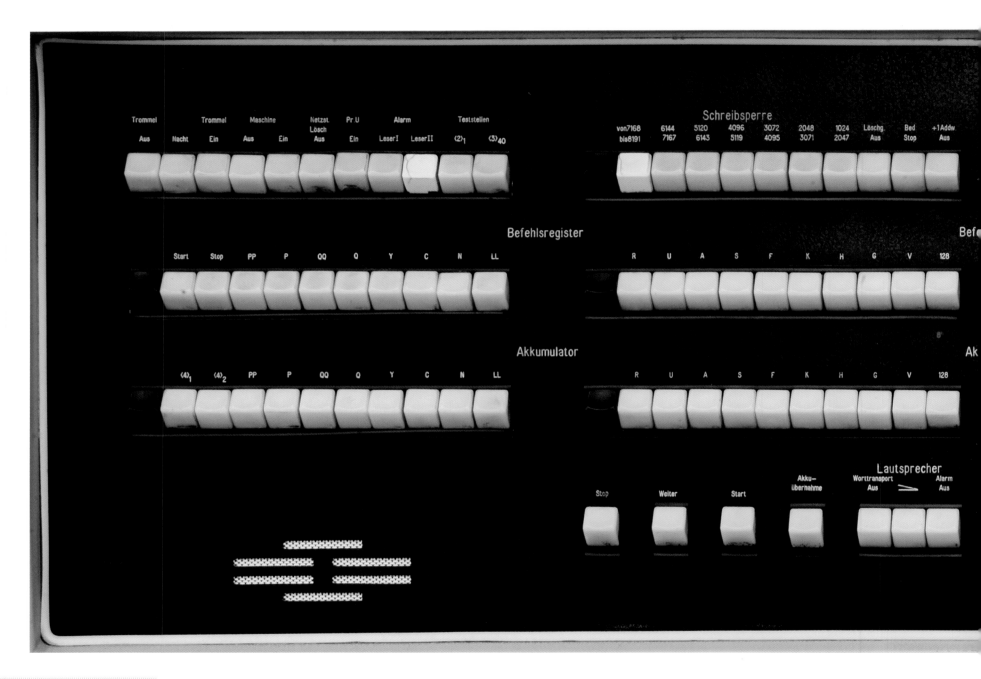

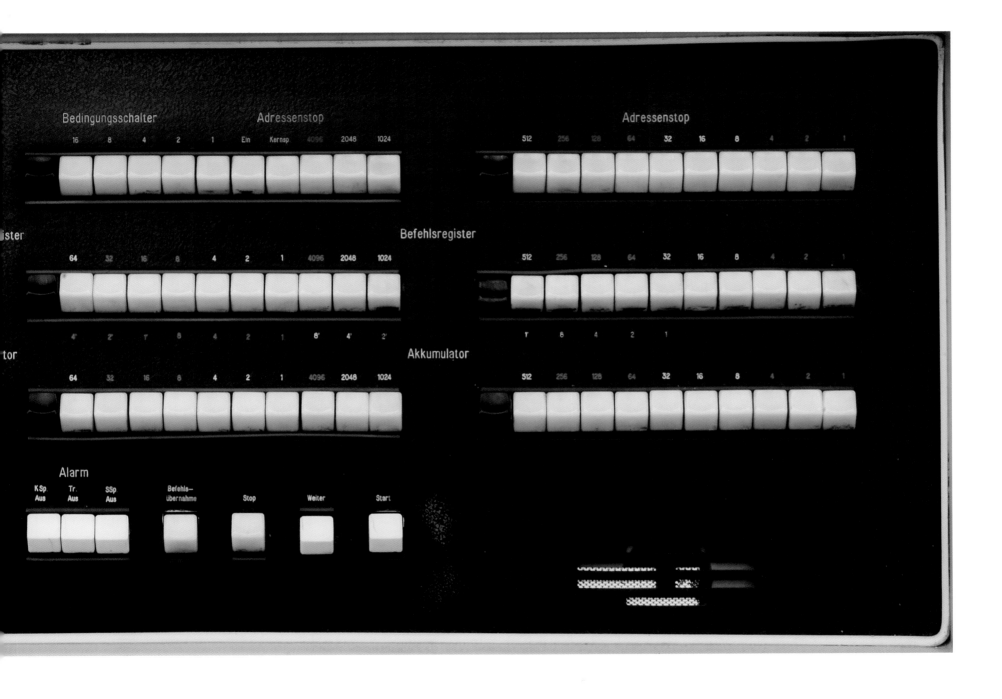

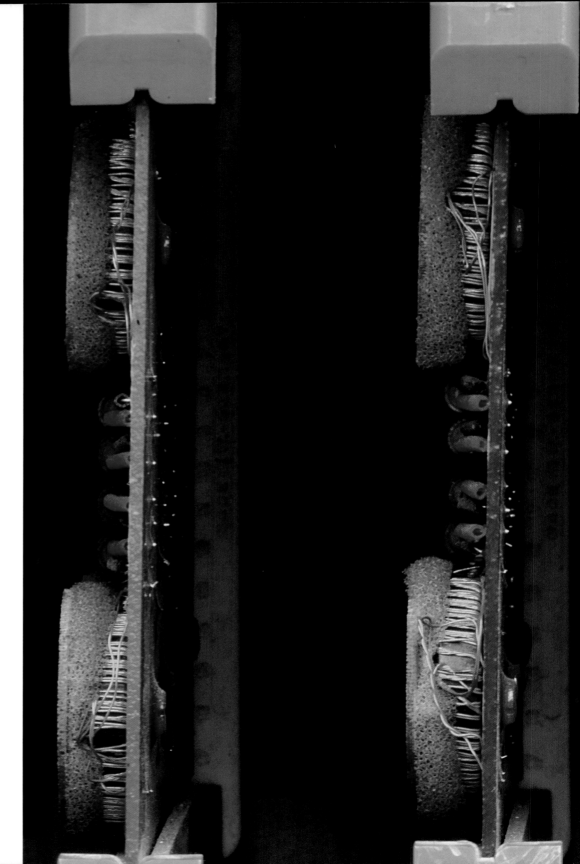

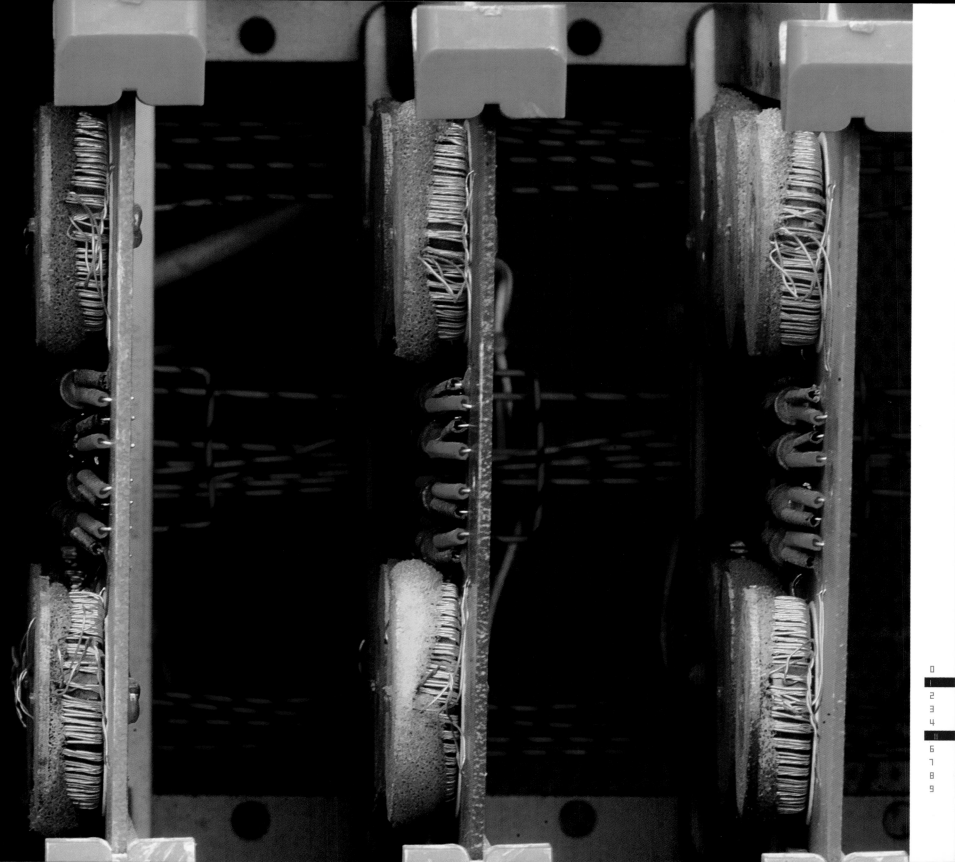

NAME	# ENIAC (ELECTRONIC NUMERICAL INTEGRATOR AND COMPUTER)
YEAR CREATED	1946
CREATOR	U.S. ARMY AND MOORE SCHOOL OF ENGINEERING, UNIVERSITY OF PENNSYLVANIA
COST	APPROX. $500,000
MEMORY	20 TEN-DIGIT NUMBERS

..//

Though it was finished in early 1946—after Nagasaki's mushroom cloud ended the fighting—the Electronic Numerical Integrator and Computer, ENIAC, was a product of World War II and that conflict's creation of a desperate, ever-spiraling drive to outdo the opponent technologically. While the Manhattan Project feverishly completed work on the atom bomb, another effort at the University of Pennsylvania's Moore School of Engineering brought together young electrical engineer J. Presper Eckert, physicist John Mauchly, U.S. Army Captain and ballistics expert Herman H. Goldstine, and, later, the renowned mathematician John von Neumann to create a fantastic machine of forty separate eight-foot-high racks, eighteen thousand tubes, and more, at a cost of about five hundred thousand dollars.

The impetus for creating a machine with significant calculation power was the need to create firing tables to compute ballistic trajectories. Every new weapon had to have a new booklet of tables with thousands of possible trajectories, and calculating those tables was time consuming. Creating a machine that could accomplish what was taking teams of human calculators a long time to do would speed up the adoption of new weaponry.

As interesting as ENIAC was on its own, it was perhaps most important as a test case, a working model that inspired its creators to think about what they'd best do in their next projects, the EDVAC and UNIVAC. Because ENIAC could not store programs, each time a new task was required, the machine had to be physically reconfigured, so it became clear that a method for storing programs was called for. From the EDVAC came a preliminary report from von Neumann summarizing the stored program concept that grew out of the ENIAC and EDVAC work of Eckert and Mauchly. Taken together, and broadly explained by von Neumann, this work resulted in the logical basis for the computer as we know it today.

0
1
2
3
4
5
6
7
8
9

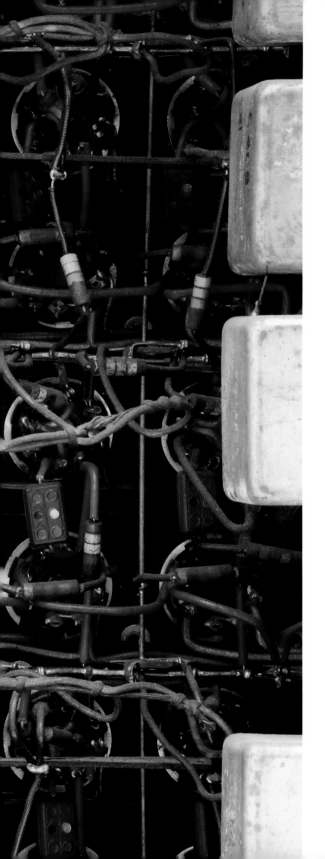

ENIAC (ELECTRONIC NUMERICAL
INTEGRATOR AND COMPUTER), 1946

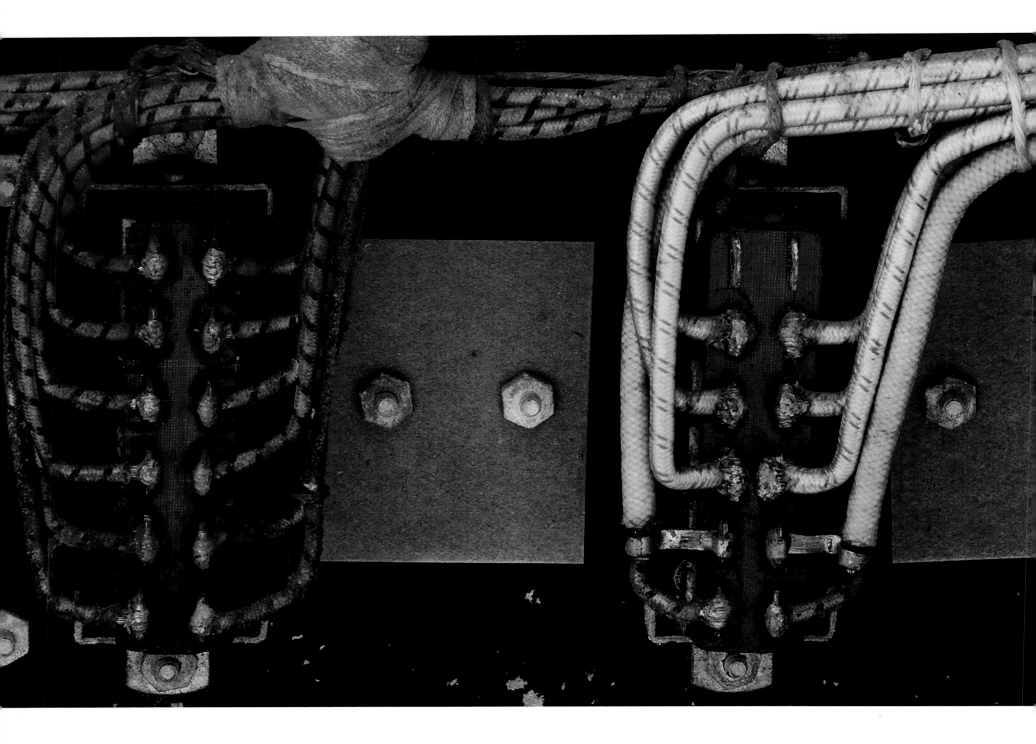

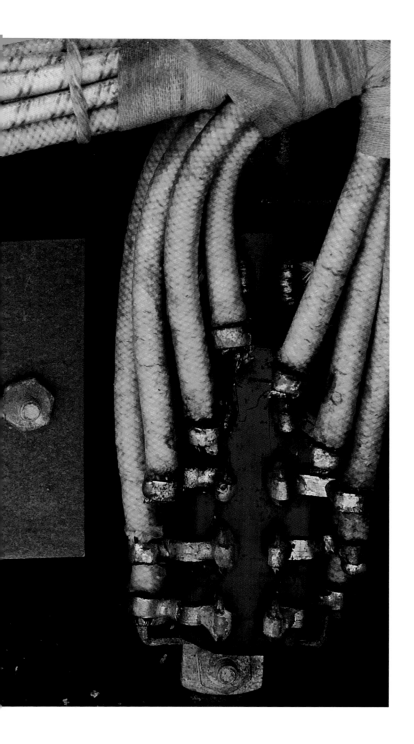

ENIAC (ELECTRONIC NUMERICAL
INTEGRATOR AND COMPUTER), 1946

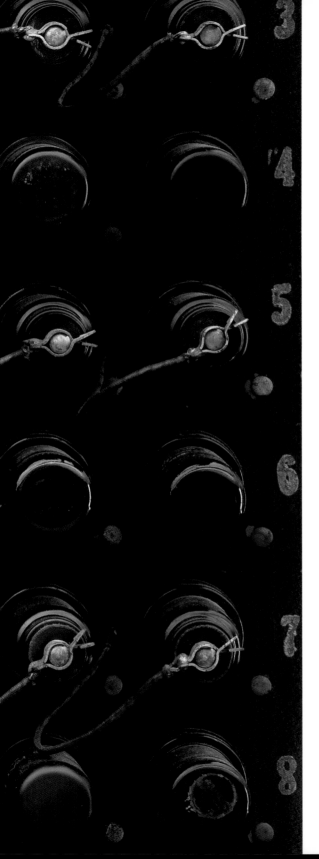

ENIAC (ELECTRONIC NUMERICAL
INTEGRATOR AND COMPUTER), 1946

NAME	# UNIVAC I
YEAR CREATED	1951
CREATOR	REMINGTON-RAND, UNIVAC DIVISION
COST	$300,000
MEMORY	20K, MERCURY DELAY LINE

The UNIVAC (short for UNIVersal Automatic Computer) was the first commercial computer in the United States. The UNIVAC I was aimed at business customers and government agencies that needed to process a lot of data for applications such as commerce and census work.

The computer was built by J. Presper Eckert and John Mauchly, who were both fresh from their experience with the ENIAC and possessed a clear vision of how stored-program computers should work. Mauchly and Eckert had initially tried to produce the UNIVAC at their own company, the Eckert-Mauchly Computer Corporation, but when building the machine for the Census Bureau went well over the three-hundred-thousand-dollar budget originally agreed upon, and the bureau would not pay any more, Eckert-Mauchly was sold, eventually to Remington-Rand, which thereby got the historical credit for releasing the first commercial computer in the U.S.

For main memory the UNIVAC used a huge mercury delay line—pictured here—and tape drives were used to store programs and data. To process information, the mercury delay line used sound waves to send pulses through a tube of mercury, then detect and return them. This memory tank would hold eighteen such tubes. The use of tape, rather than punch cards, to store information was a significant innovation and one that was met with significant resistance from customers who would no longer see and hold data in hand, as they had with punch cards. Adding to the anxiety, salesmen from competitor IBM were said to have suggested that the spinning metal tape posed a safety hazard.

It was the Census Bureau that ordered the first UNIVAC; General Electric was the first commercial customer, obtaining serial number 8, in 1953. The UNIVAC garnered a lot of publicity when it was used to predict election results in 1952 from a small sample of voters in key states. It accurately predicted Eisenhower's landslide victory over Adlai Stevenson and helped further solidify the hopes and fears that the general public had about these wondrous but scary machines.

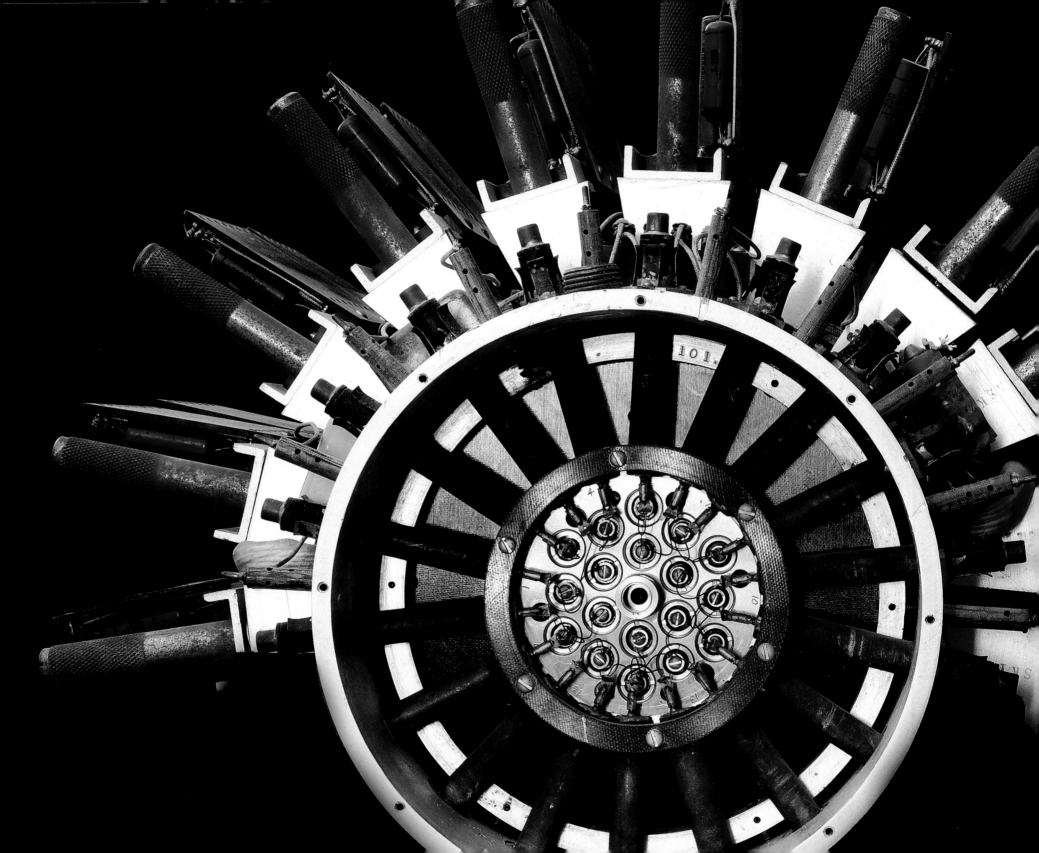

UNIVAC I, 1951

NAME	# WISC (WISCONSIN INTEGRALLY SYNCHRONIZED COMPUTER)
YEAR CREATED	1955
CREATOR	GENE AMDAHL, UNIVERSITY OF WISCONSIN
COST	$50,000 (ESTIMATE)
MEMORY	1K, MAGNETIC DRUM

..//

Gene Amdahl, a theoretical physics student, needed to have more computing power if he was going to be able to move ahead with his research. So, as his Ph.D. project at the University of Wisconsin, he designed the Wisconsin Integrally Synchronized Computer, or WISC. Using magnetic-drum-based memory (the pictured switch controls the speed of the drum, driving the speed of the system), WISC looked a little unusual but was similar in function to its contemporaries, if a little bare-bones. But it was, after all, 1955, and features such as an obviously appropriated standard metal desk accentuate just how unique computers were then.

Apart from the fact that it's the only computer at the museum to be punctured by bullet holes, what is particularly notable about the WISC is that its designer, Amdahl, was to go on to be an important figure in the world of computers: he worked on the IBM Model 7030 (Stretch), was architect of the IBM System/360, and articulated the FUD concept (Fear, Uncertainty, and Doubt — the marketing principle of spreading negative but unspecific information about a competitor's product), as well as Amdahl's Law, the basis for projecting performance in parallel processing. When he left IBM in 1970 to found the Amdahl Corporation in Sunnyvale, California, Amdahl brought large-scale computer design to what would become Silicon Valley.

After Amdahl was finished with it, the WISC machine was used primarily by other University of Wisconsin students to learn about computing, then abandoned years later, after which it suffered a few injuries as the result of someone's wayward target practice.

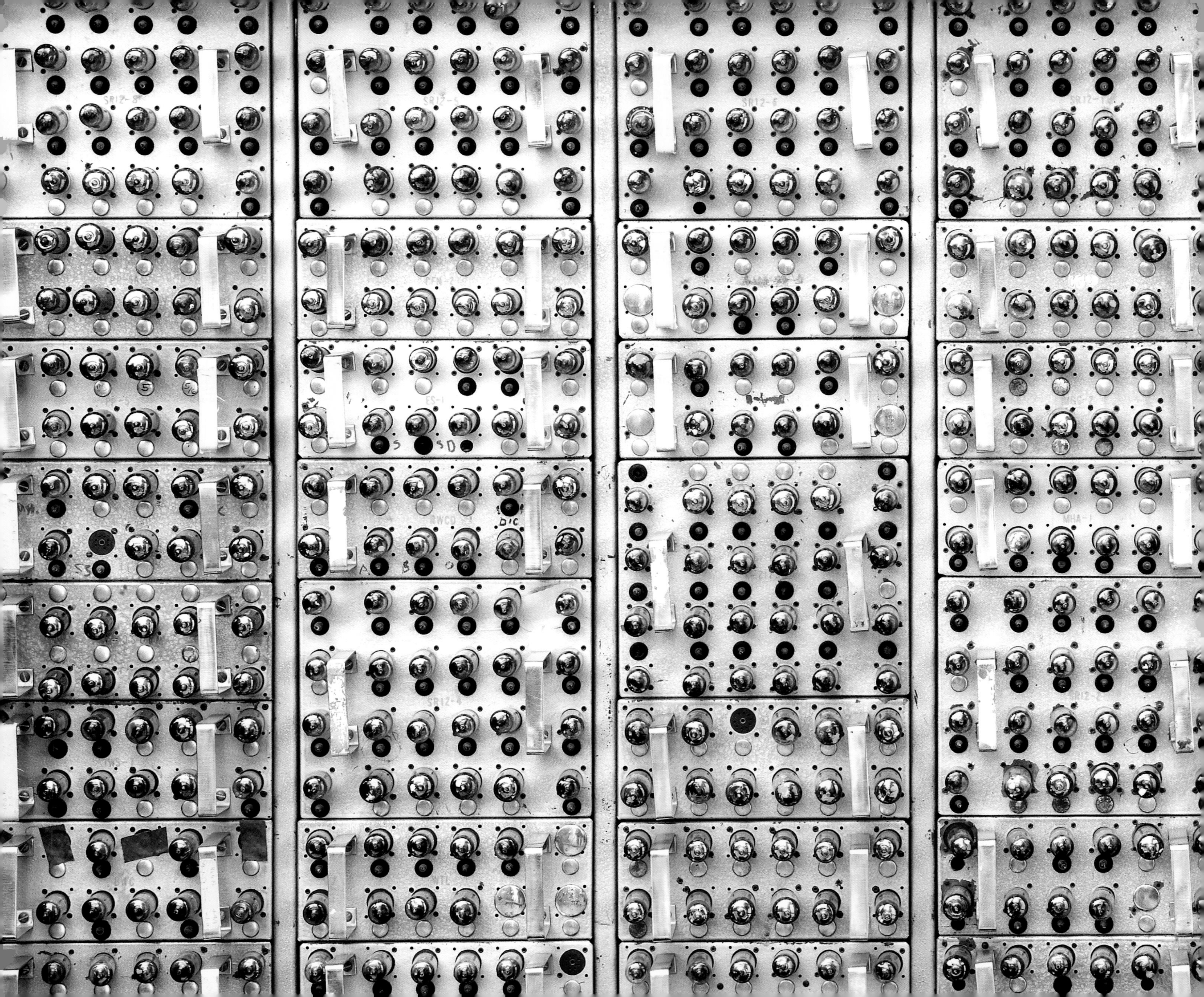

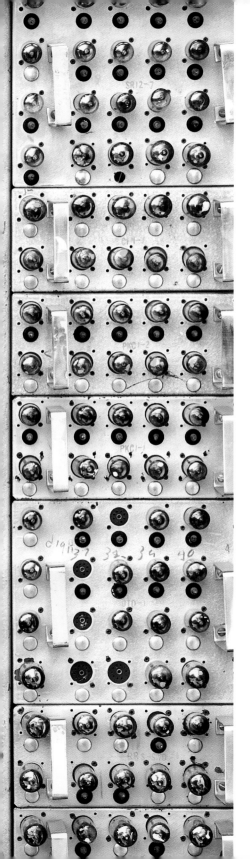

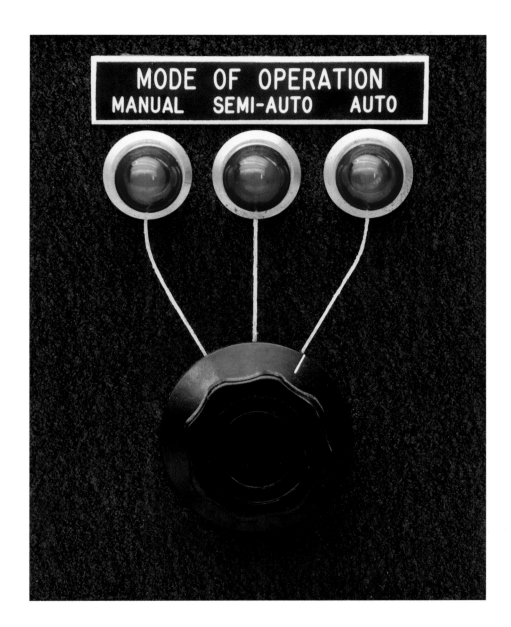

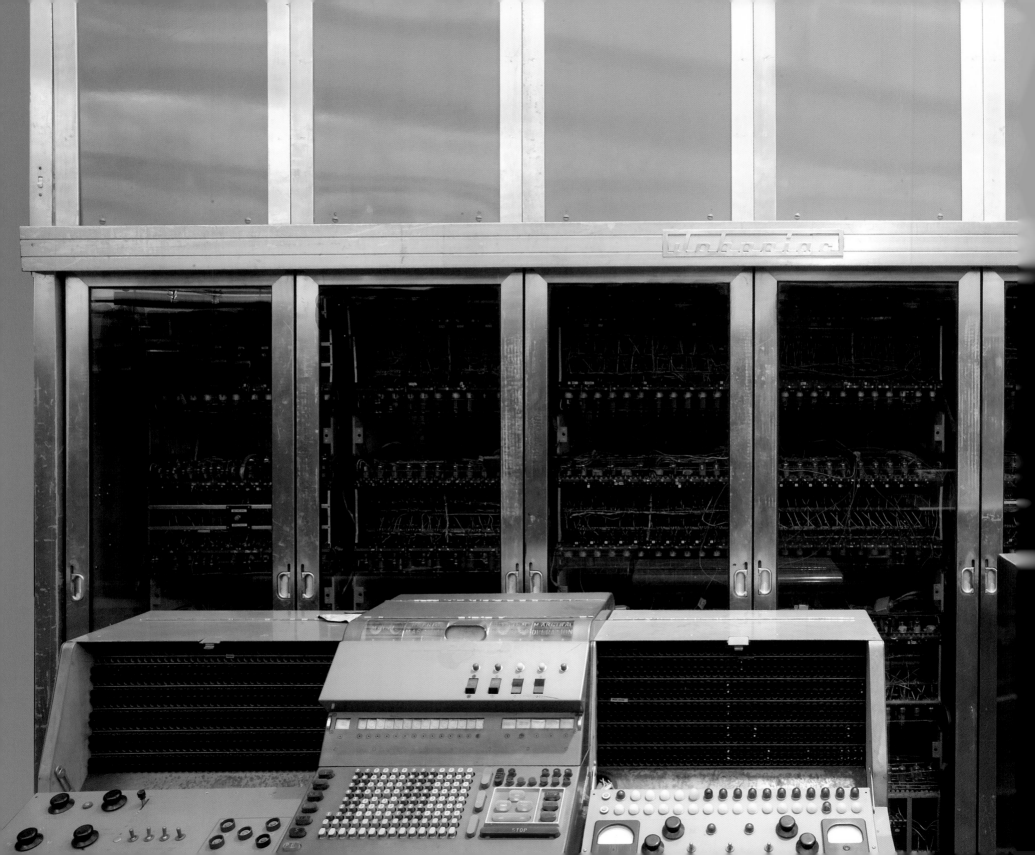

NAME	JOHNNIAC
YEAR CREATED	1954
CREATOR	RAND CORPORATION
COST	$470,000
MEMORY	4K CORE

The Johnniac was a one-of-a-kind computer built by Rand, based on the theories of John von Neumann and, despite his weak protests, named in his honor.

After von Neumann wrote his "First Draft of a Report on the EDVAC" and coauthored several other reports—such as his "Preliminary Discussion of the Logical Design of an Electronic Computing Instrument," in which he articulated the principles of stored program computing, later to be defined as "von Neumann Architecture"—he went on to direct the construction of the IAS machine at Princeton's Institute for Advanced Study, in 1952.

The IAS machine was an inspiration to computer makers, and a series of seventeen versions of the machine (whose plans were freely available) were built at various places around the world. The machines were known collectively as "IAS machines," and many took playful variations on a theme as their names: the MANIAC, the SILLIAC, and the WEIZAC. Though they were based on similar principles, these computers were one-of-a-kind machines, and though they all could store programs, they could not share the programs with one another.

The Johnniac was used to crunch numbers for payroll and mathematics, but it was also programmed to play a game of chess. It used a keyboard as its terminal (which looked simply like an old laboratory-green typewriter) and used a time-sharing operating system based on minutes, rather than the microseconds that would later be common. It initially used an expensive experimental memory known as the Selectron but was upgraded to magnetic core memory in 1954.

This Johnniac is the only complete IAS-type machine, except for the original, known to still exist.

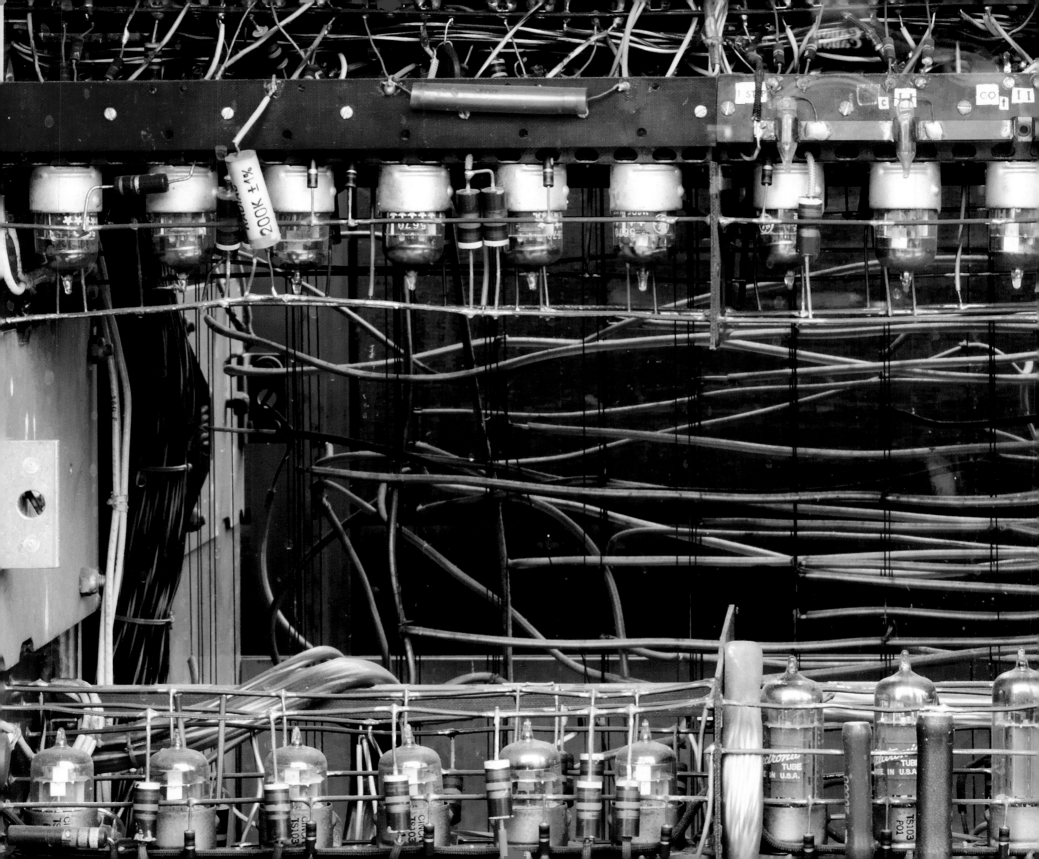

0
1
2

4
5
6 ||

8
9

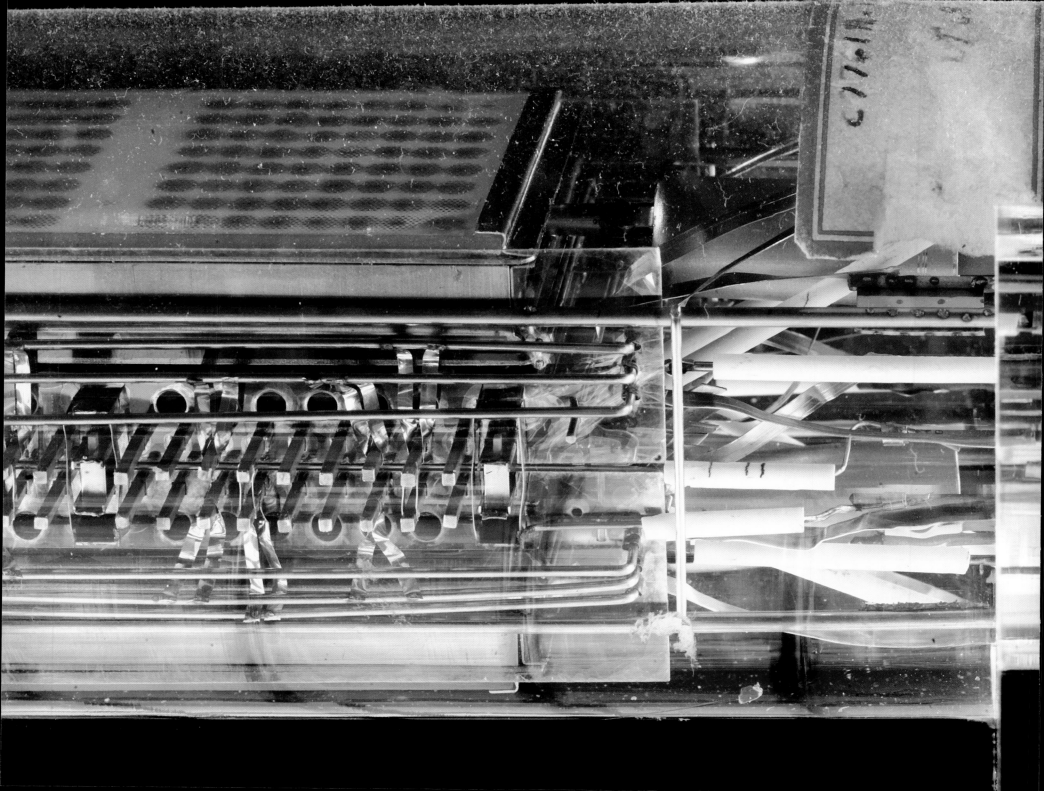

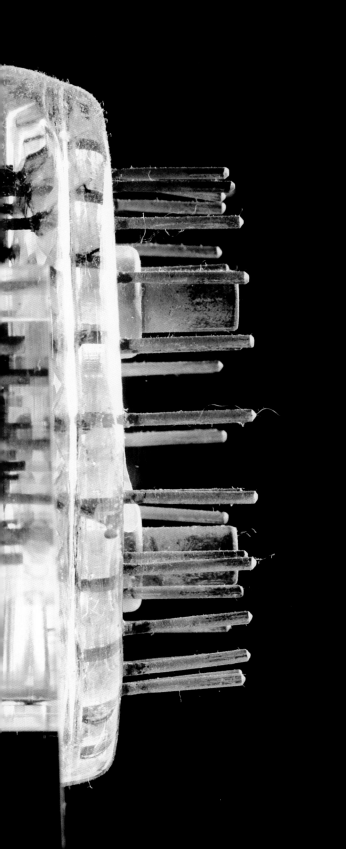

0
1
2
4
5
6
7
8
11

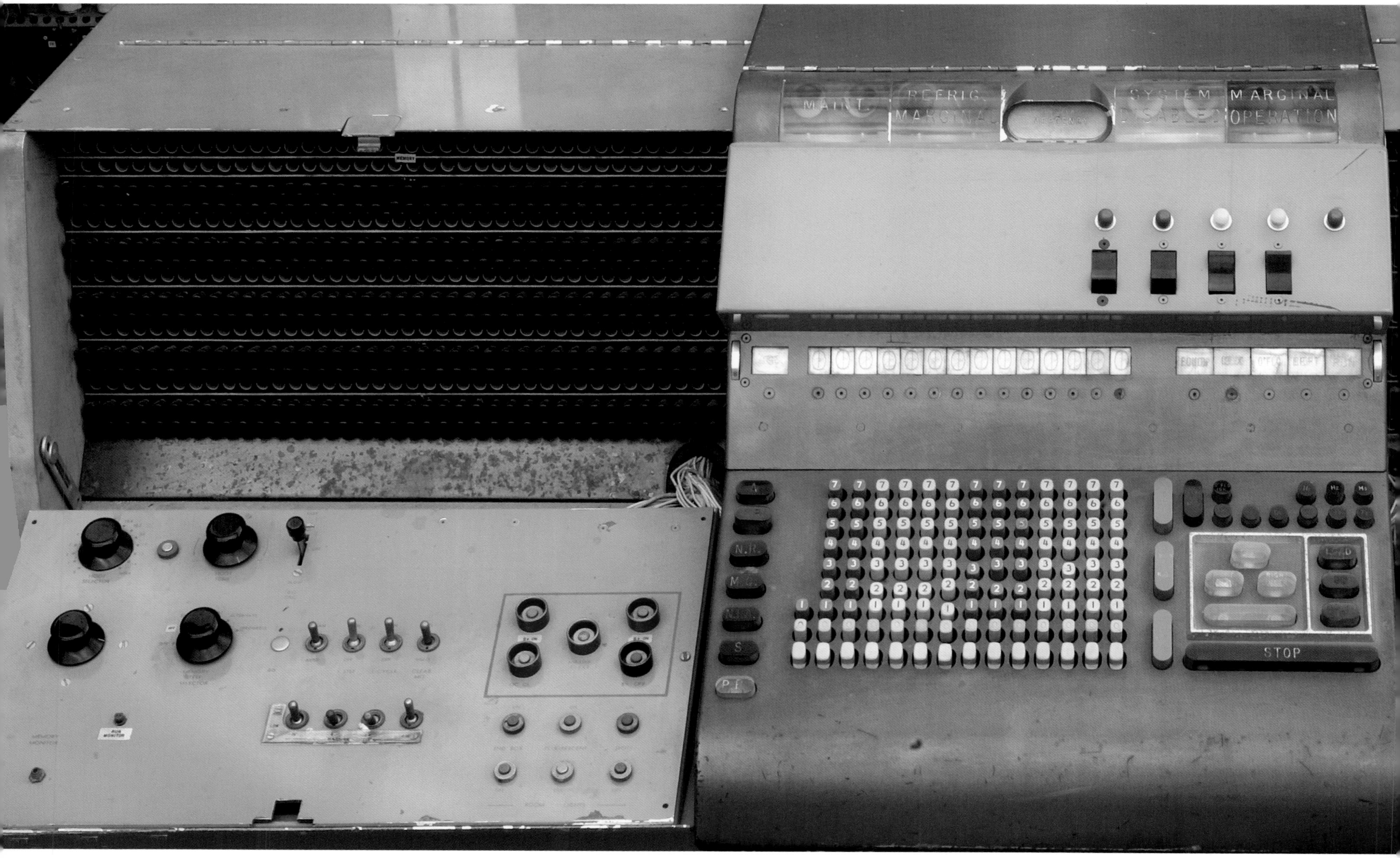
MAINT
REFRIG. MARGINAL
SYSTEM DISABLED
MARGINAL OPERATION
STOP

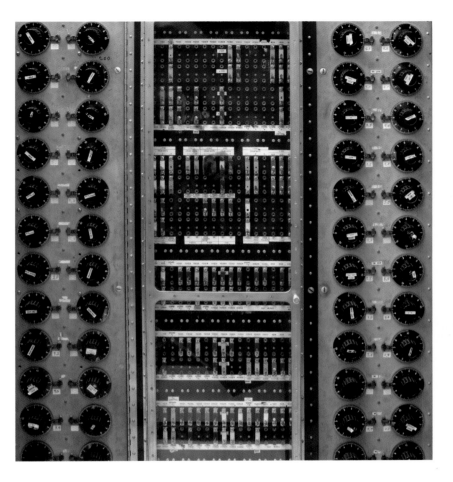

CORE MEMORY

..//

Before magnetic core memory, there were several types of main memories used in computers: drum memory, delay lines, electrostatic storage, vacuum tubes, and relays. All had their strengths for certain applications (like radar) but none was reliable enough for use in a computer. By combining the pioneering research done at Harvard by An Wang and Way Dong-Wu with their own, Jay Forrester's researchers at MIT were able to create magnetic core memory for the Whirlwind computer, which became the basis for the influential SAGE air-defense system.

As its name suggests, magnetic core memory is a magnetic force that drives the ability of rings and wires to store information. Cores are the actual rings of ferrite that are held suspended in a grid of wires. The components work together so that a charge is delivered to one of the points on the grid where a ring sits and magnetizes that ring in a clockwise or counter-clockwise direction, corresponding to a one or a zero: one bit. By combining several layers of these grids, or planes, a stack is made. Other variations were developed, but this was the basic principle.

Core memory is able to hold its state, thus retaining information even when its electricity supply is turned off. Because of this "nonvolatility" and the benefit that any point of information is as easy and quick to access as any other point in the core plane, core memory quickly caught on, and it became the standard until it was replaced by the integrated circuit.

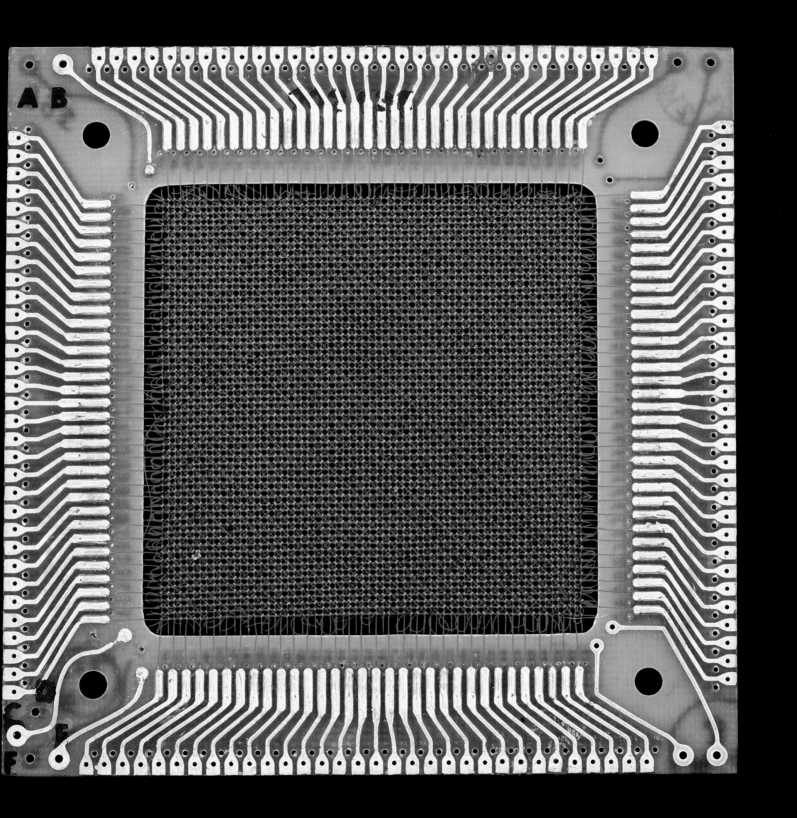

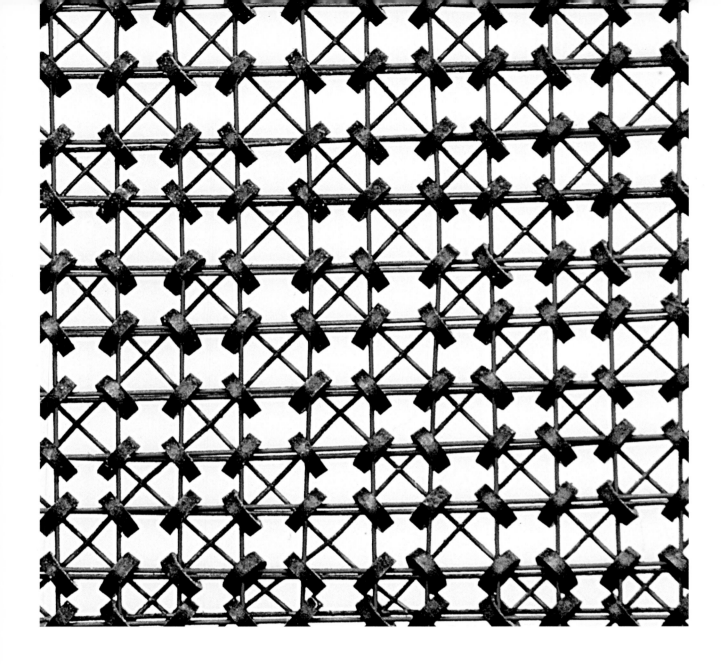

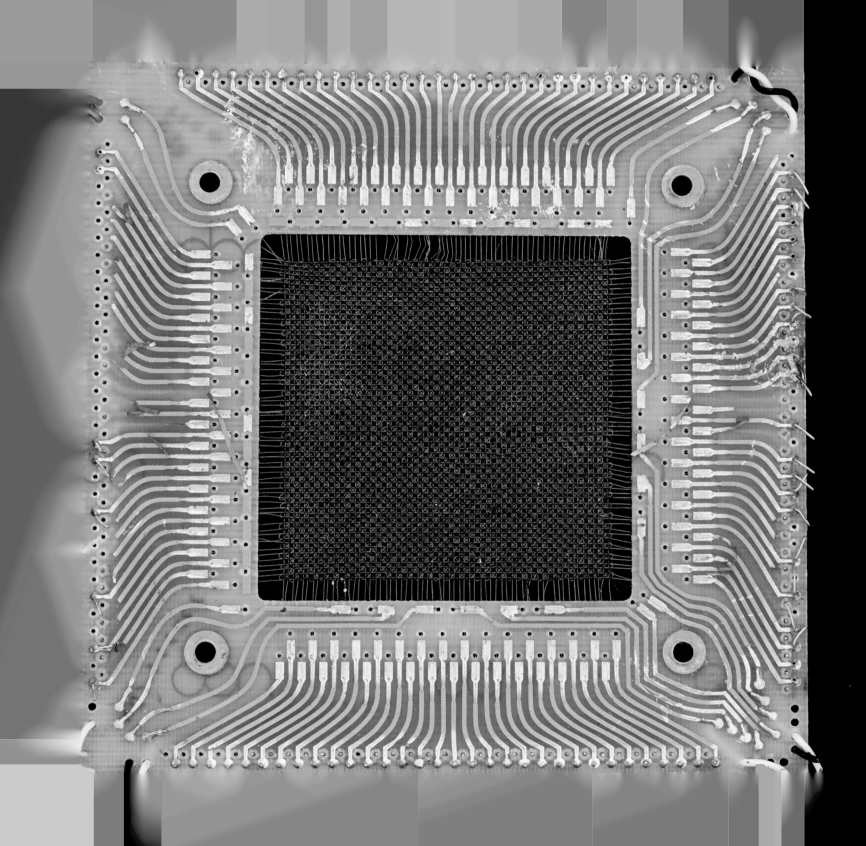

NAME	SAGE (SEMI-AUTOMATIC GROUND ENVIRONMENT)
YEAR CREATED	1954–63
CREATOR	UNITED STATES AIR FORCE, IBM, WESTERN ELECTRICS, SDC
COST	$8 BILLION TO $12 BILLION (ESTIMATED COST FOR ENTIRE SYSTEM)
MEMORY	69 KW CORE

SAGE (SEMI-AUTOMATIC GROUND ENVIRONMENT)

..//

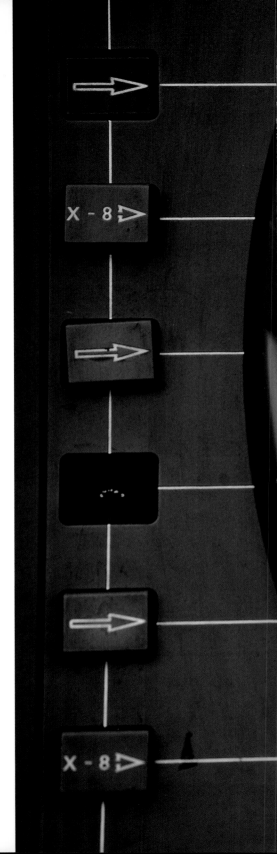

Foremost among the early cold-war fears of Americans was the threat of a Soviet air invasion. To assuage the collective worries and provide for the common defense, the U.S. Air Force created the Semi-Automatic Ground Environment, or SAGE, a network of large, innovative computers that would collect and analyze radar data in real time and communicate the pertinent data to fighter planes.

The heart of the SAGE system was based on MIT's Whirlwind (1951), the first computer built for real-time interactivity and the first user of core memory. IBM was contracted to build the hardware for the system, which also included such important innovations as display monitors, modems, and networking. Rand was in charge of writing the immense software of two hundred fifty thousand lines — and employed seven thousand programmers to get the job done. The footprint was also enormous: one installation would take up four floors of a building half the size of a football field (two systems were placed at each installation to ensure backup), and fifty-three thousand vacuum tubes were used for an individual SAGE computer.

It wasn't just the individual technical pieces that set SAGE apart. The complexity of a system that linked twenty-seven computer installations, radar, aircraft, and ships to deliver a graphic picture of the state of the nation's skies was a vast exercise in collecting, processing, and envisioning information in real time. The implications were far reaching both for hardware and software development, and for the practical experience of interpreting such a large amount of data.

Thankfully, an invasion such as it was built to detect never took place, and the SAGE system's descendants tracked friendlier skies as reservation systems for the airline industry. The light gun used in the SAGE system also developed a more peaceable form, morphing into the light pen. IBM gained a lot of expertise, as well as prestige, implementing the system for NORAD and was able to use much of what it learned to build business machines.

An innovation that we don't see anymore in today's computers is a built-in cigarette lighter and ashtray. Most SAGE installations were in remote areas, in bunkers some six hundred feet underground. A few vices were allowed.

SAGE (SEMI-AUTOMATIC GROUND ENVIRONMENT), 1961

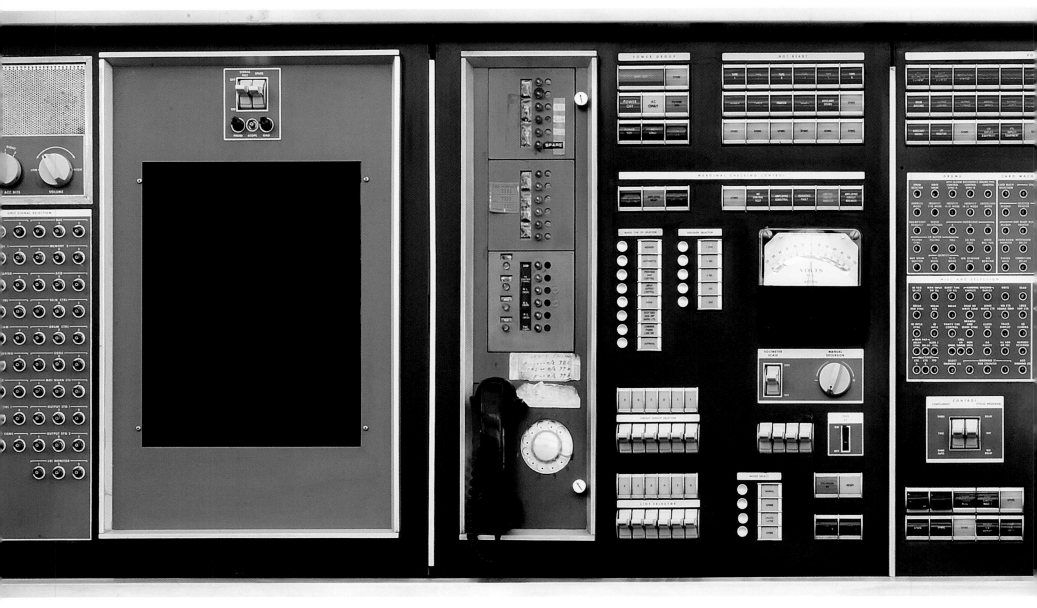

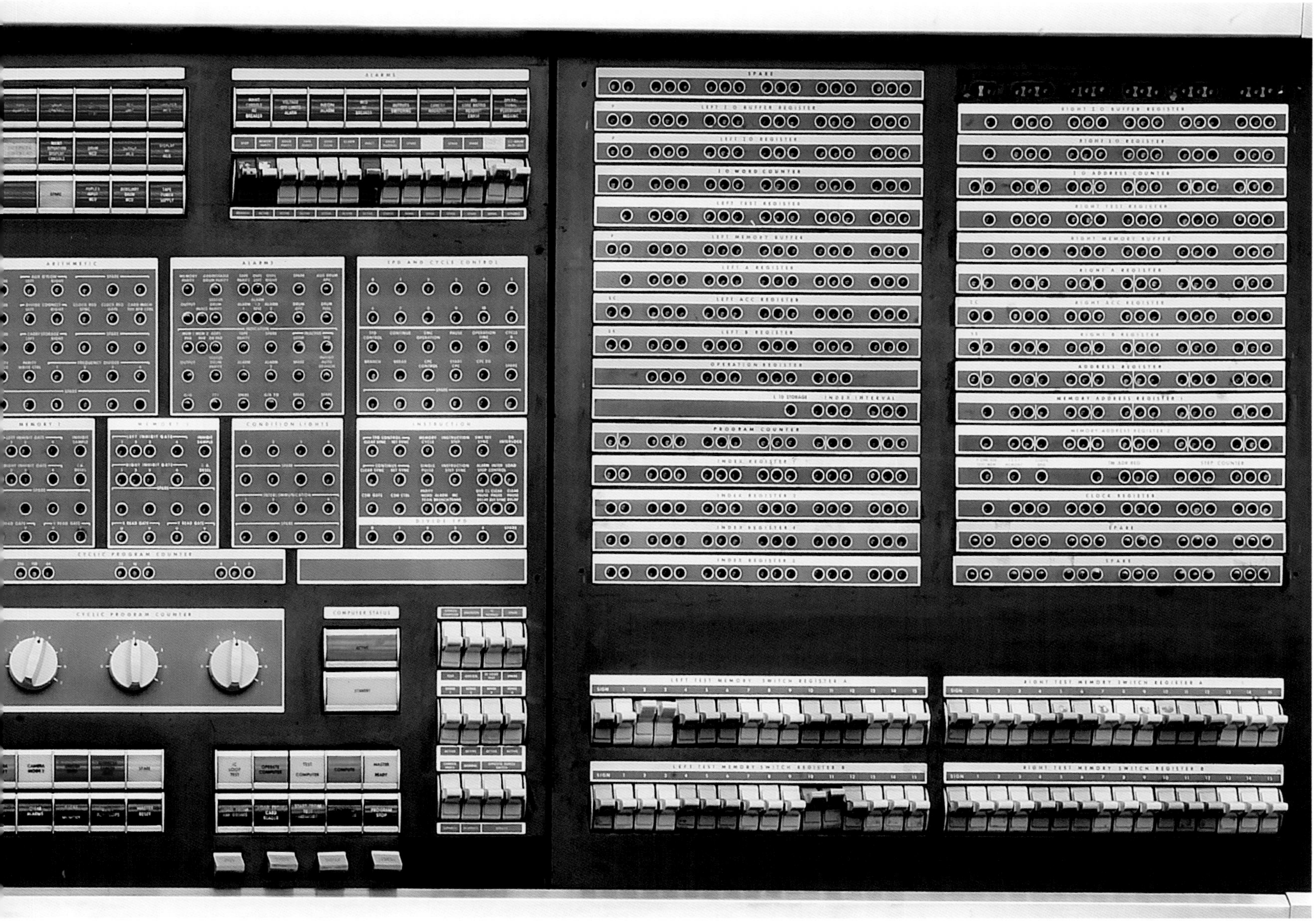

SAGE (SEMI-AUTOMATIC
GROUND ENVIRONMENT),
1961

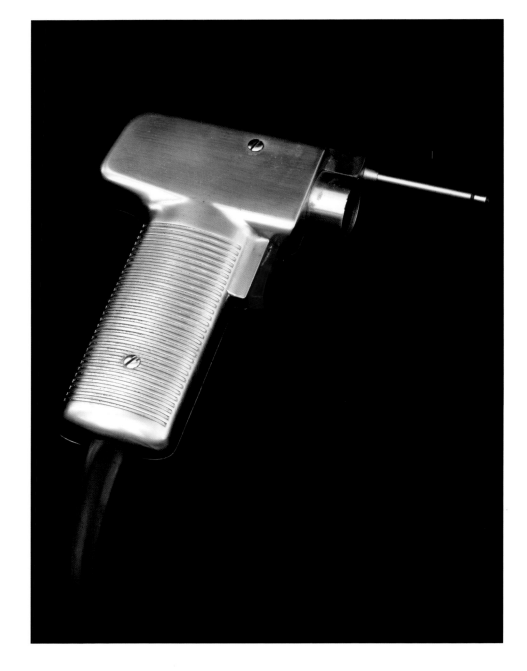

SAGE (SEMI-AUTOMATIC ∧ >
GROUND ENVIRONMENT),
1961

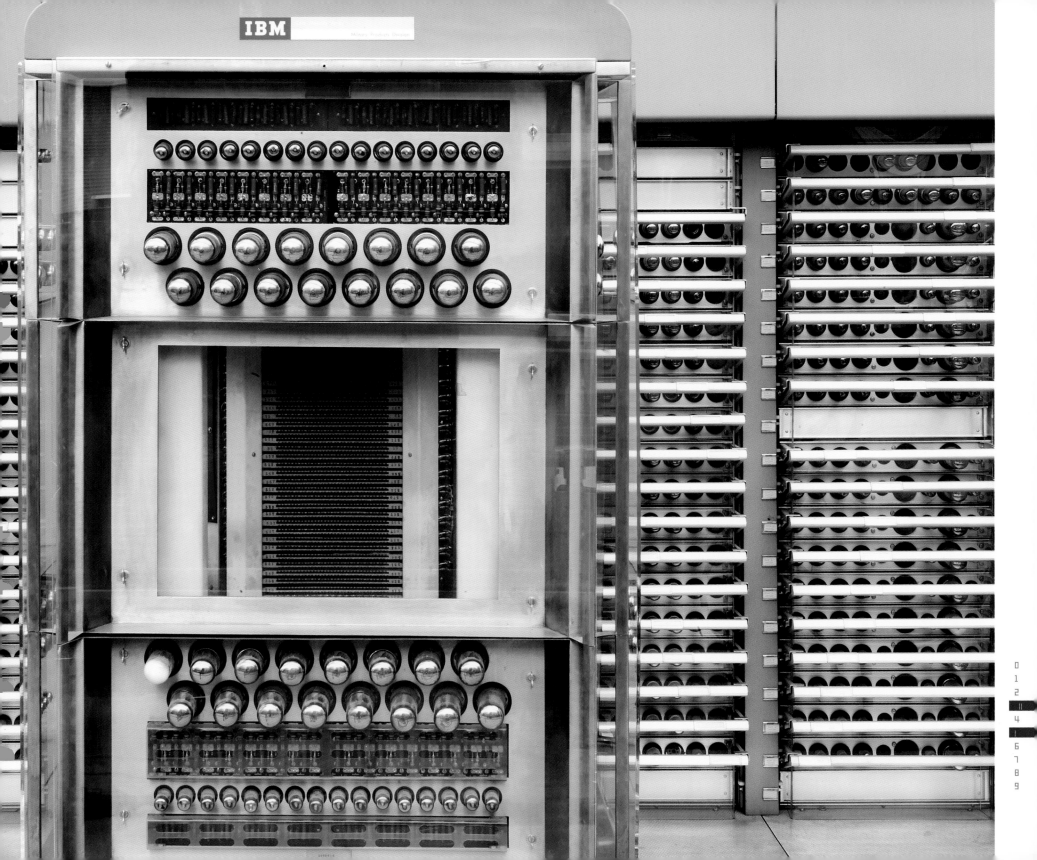

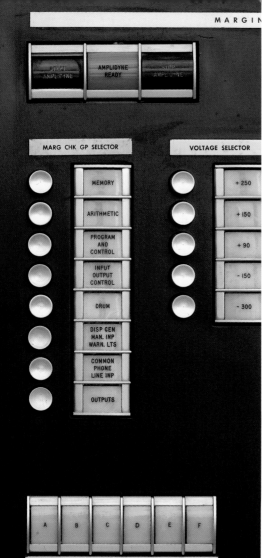

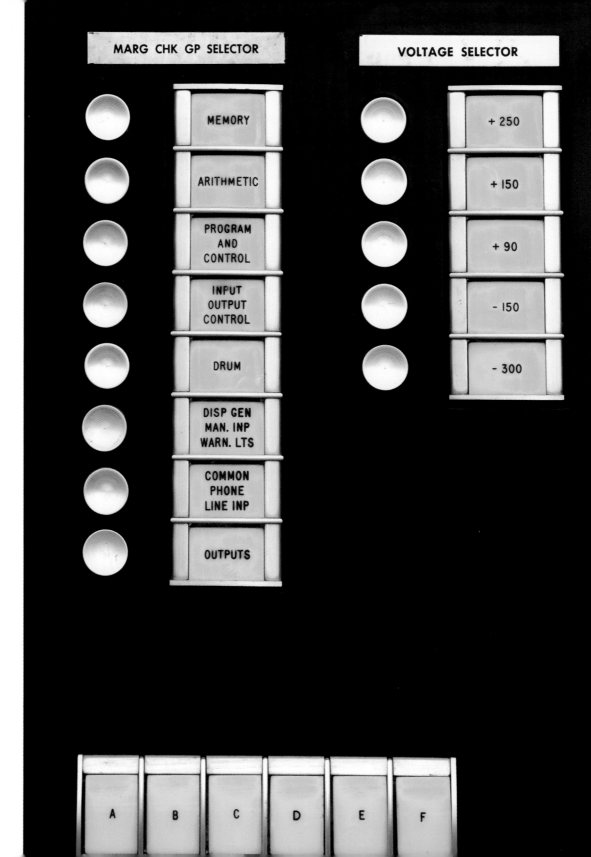

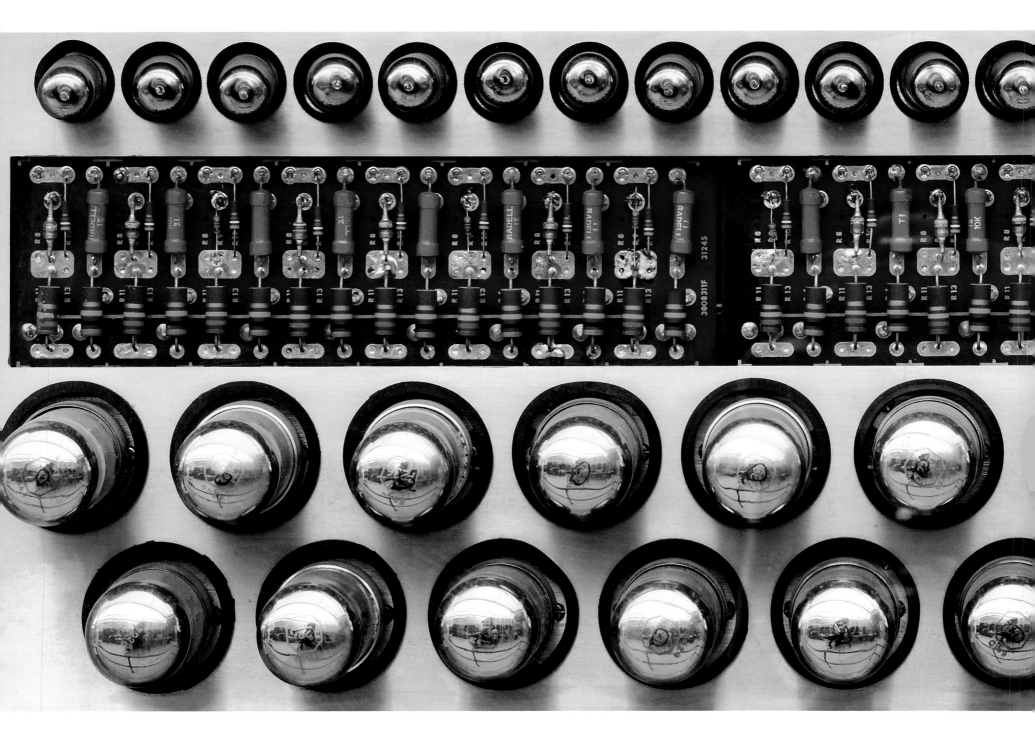

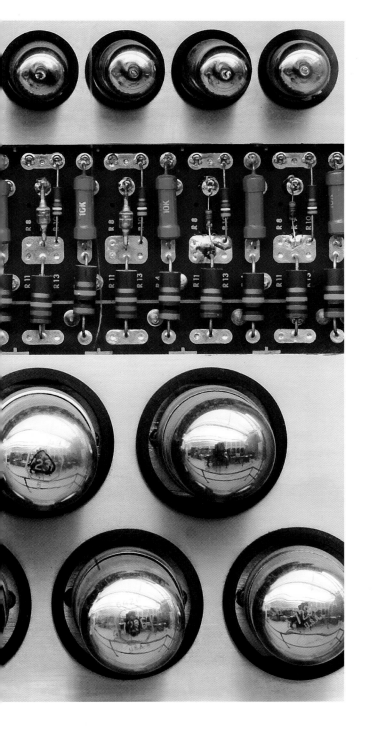

SAGE (SEMI-AUTOMATIC
GROUND ENVIRONMENT),
1961

NAME	**NEAC 2203**
YEAR CREATED	1960
CREATOR	NIPPON ELECTRIC COMPANY (NEC)
COST	¥27,643,000
MEMORY	DRUM 2,040 BITS

../ /

This Nippon Electric Company, or Nippon Denki Kabushiki Gaisha, knew how to make a cool-looking, utilitarian-chic computer, and in the old days the company didn't seem to mind sticking its equipment on top of a regular green metal desk. With a solid-state design (its predecessor, the 2201, was the first NEC transistorized machine) and many standard features of the era (paper-tape entry and punch, magnetic tape storage, drum memory), the NEAC 2203 also could use the characters from either the Roman alphabet or the Japanese *kana* syllabary (though not the much larger set of *kanji* characters).

NEC, founded in 1899, was the first joint Japanese-American company in Japan. Despite the heavy toll taken on Japan's infrastructure by World War II, NEC continued its work in communication technology and entered the transistor market in 1950. It began computer research four years later, finally releasing its first computer, the NEAC 1101, in 1958.

MINUTEMAN I
GUIDANCE COMPUTER

NAME	MINUTEMAN I GUIDANCE COMPUTER
YEAR CREATED	1962
CREATOR	AUTONETICS FOR THE UNITED STATES AIR FORCE
MEMORY	2,560 WORDS, MAGNETIC DISK

Autonetics, a division of North American Aviation, built this 24-bit serial minicomputer to control the onboard guidance system of the Minuteman I Intercontinental Ballistic Missile (ICBM). The Minuteman system was a vast installation of underground silos, each holding a nuclear-tipped missile that was designed to be launched in the event that the cold war turned hot.

How do you make sure your nuclear missile can find its way to its destination even when the atmosphere through which it's flying has been disrupted by atomic explosions? The answer for the Minuteman I was to jettison (figuratively) the standard radio-transmitter-based link to earthbound computer guidance in favor of having the missile carry its own navigational computer. The new system had to be small enough to fit onboard and overcome the problem that radio control was unreliable over long distances. It used a magnetic disk, like a primitive version of today's hard disks, for active memory, making it a little slow, but inexpensive and reliable.

The missile's successor, the Minuteman II, would later be one of the driving forces behind the adoption of the integrated circuit, making the IC's mass production by Texas Instruments and others feasible.

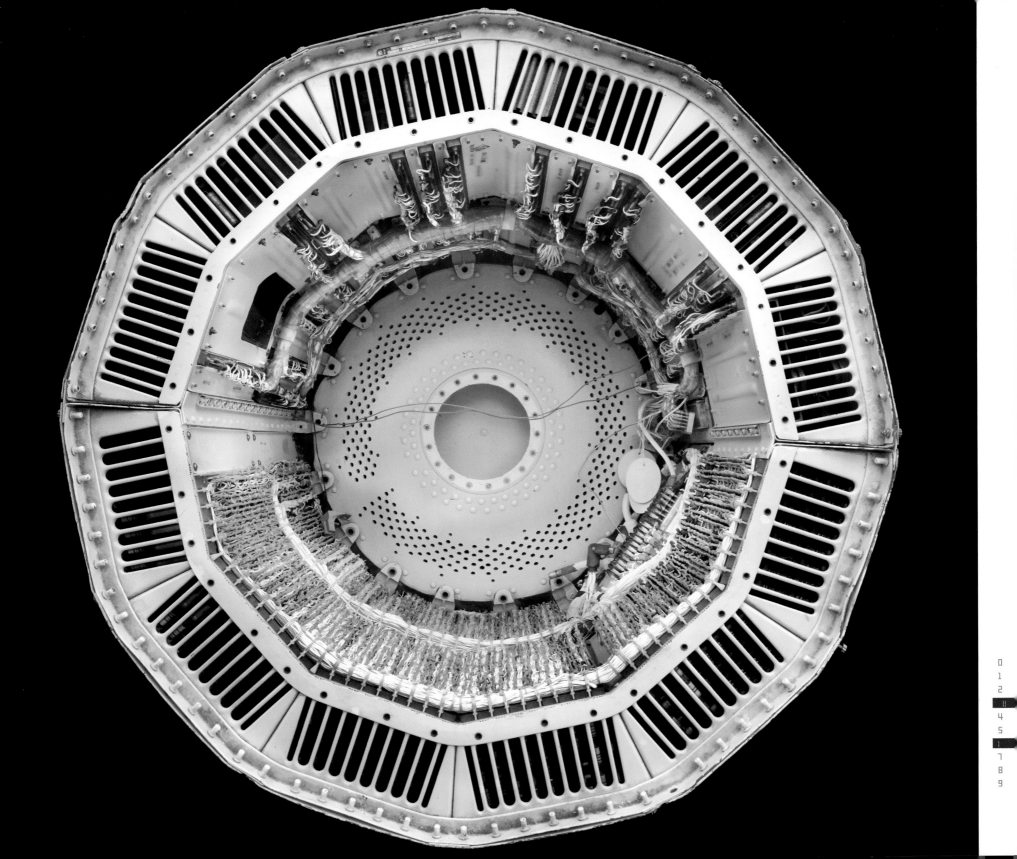

NAME	PHILCO 212
YEAR CREATED	1962
CREATOR	PHILCO CORPORATION
COST	$1.8 MILLION
MEMORY	64K

.://

Philco, short for the Philadelphia Electric Company, was an early manufacturer of transistors, and in the late 1950s it was one of the largest. Philco had a long history with radio and television, and its designs were often quite striking, including the archetype of 1930s radio, the vaguely gothic wooden receiver, and the icon of 1950s television, the futuristic Predicta, which featured a tiltable picture tube held separately from its receiver base.

Since the company's transistors were essential to making computers, it seemed quite natural that Philco should make its own. Its first computer, the SOLO, was built for the National Security Agency and was among the first transistor-driven computers. Although transistor manufacturers like Philco were among the first to enter the computer business, they were generally not the ones that enjoyed the most lasting success, probably because the manufacturers of business machines had a more developed customer base in the business market. Even so, Philco produced some reputable machines, including the 212, made for the general scientific and data processing market and built with heavy-duty number-crunching power.

Philco was sold to Ford in 1962, just after this computer was introduced, and quickly got out of the computer business, although Ford Philco continued to make radios, mostly for Ford cars.

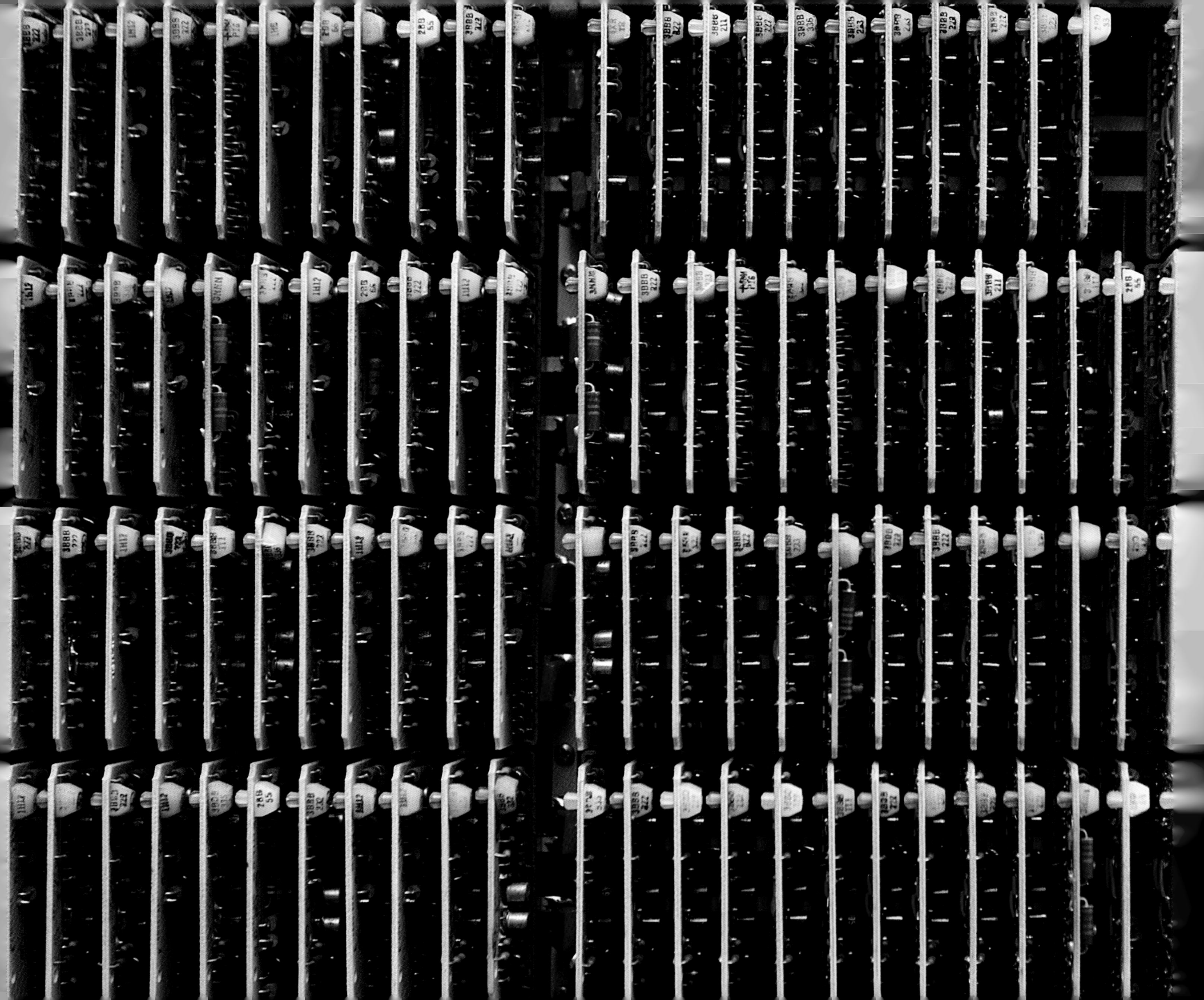

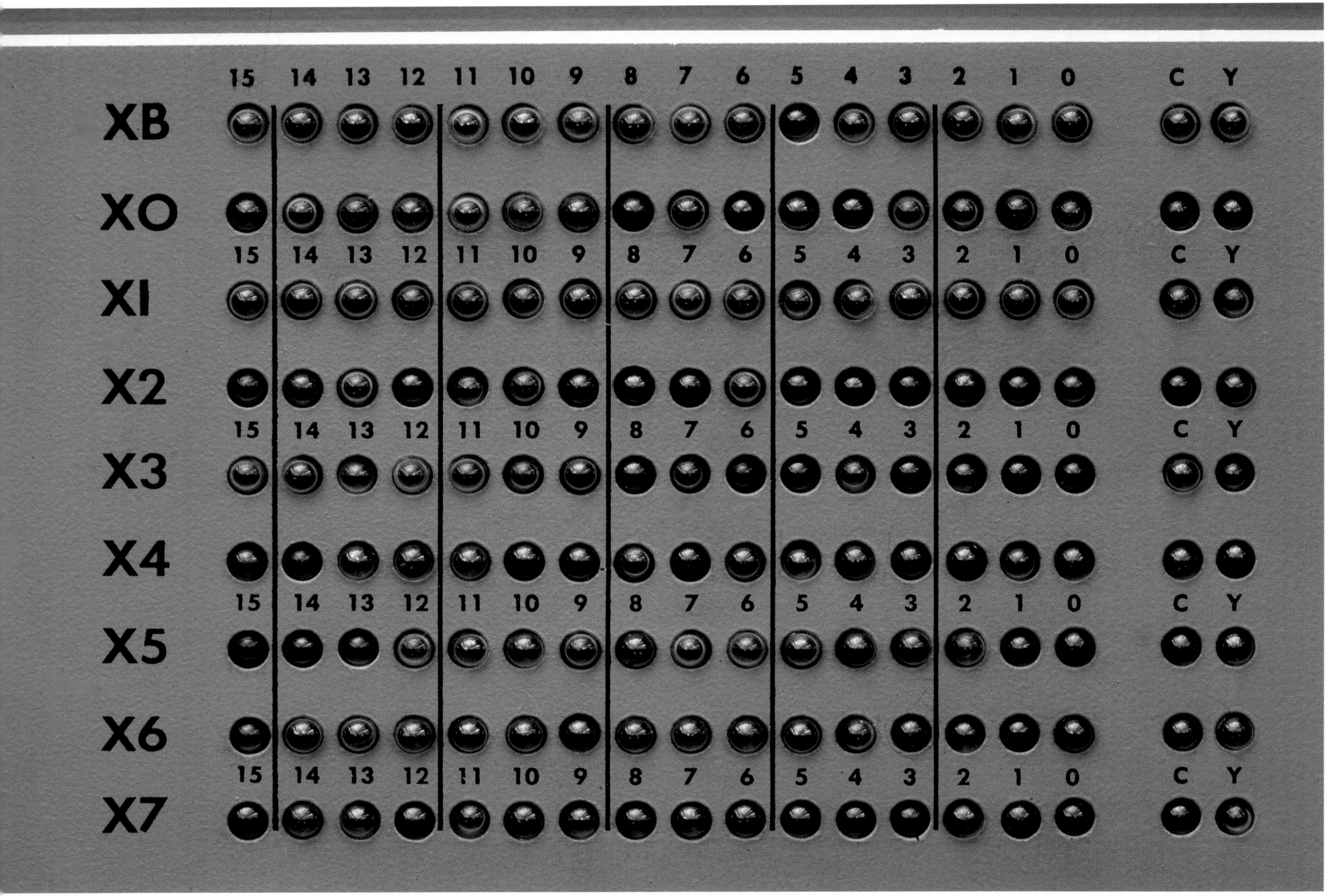
15 14 13 12 11 10 9 8 7 6 5 4 3 2 1 0 C Y
XB
XO
15 14 13 12 11 10 9 8 7 6 5 4 3 2 1 0 C Y
XI
X2
15 14 13 12 11 10 9 8 7 6 5 4 3 2 1 0 C Y
X3
X4
15 14 13 12 11 10 9 8 7 6 5 4 3 2 1 0 C Y
X5
X6
15 14 13 12 11 10 9 8 7 6 5 4 3 2 1 0 C Y
X7

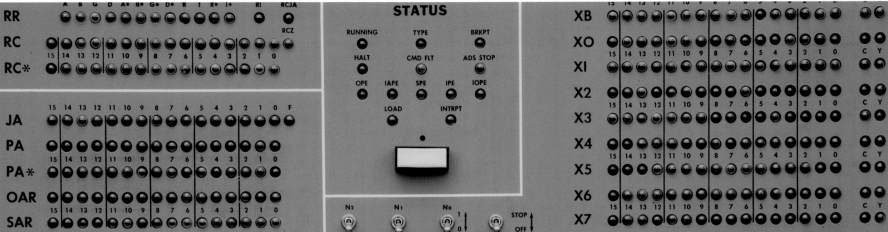

NAME	IBM SYSTEM/360
	(AND IBM 7030 "STRETCH")
YEAR CREATED	1964
CREATOR	INTERNATIONAL BUSINESS MACHINES (IBM)
COST	$133,000 AND UP
MEMORY	VARIOUS, DEPENDING ON MODEL
OPERATING SYSTEM	OS/360

The IBM System/360 was a family of intercompatible computers, the first of its kind to offer customers a chance to enlarge or shrink their stable of machinery without having to also purchase new software. Such a transition was usually the cause of a lot of headaches and expense and could paralyze a company when it came to upgrading computers, or even starting out. By making it easier to change machines, as long as those new machines were in the System/360 family, the new range gave IBM a greater lock on its customer base while also encouraging more frequent upgrades. This was clever thinking from the company whose products had the reputation of being "sold, not bought."

Although the marketing advantages were clear, the success of System/360 was also fostered by technological and simple efficiency goals. Too many hardware lines operating too many different operating systems became a swelling logistical problem for IBM; focusing on the System/360 line would make it easier for IBM to perfect and support a single system. Compatibility would reign. Although the aim was to make life easier for IBM, creating

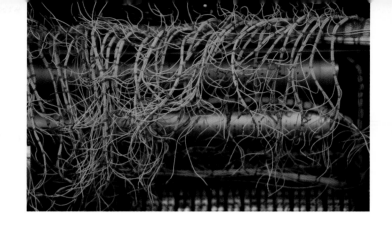

the line was a massive challenge, because before the System/360 line was built, few of IBM's computers were compatible with one another.

Several System/360 concepts were initially part of an earlier project by the computer architect Gene Amdahl: the IBM 7030, first developed for Los Alamos National Laboratory as the model called "Stretch." The Stretch was IBM's first attempt to create a supercomputer, and although the project didn't live up to some expectations, and about half of its initial orders were canceled, its role in the development of innovations like microprogramming made it ultimately worthwhile for IBM.

Central to the system was the adoption of the microprogram, stored in ROM, which allowed all models to operate using the same instructions, emulating the same essential design despite differences in architecture. As if it weren't enough of a challenge to make a line that worked as one from the top down, IBM also had to make the line perform equally well with applications for scientific and business customers. It succeeded. The System/360 team, including Gene Amdahl, pulled off the audacious venture and built the base system that would sustain IBM for decades. Higher-end System/360 models would serve as the basis for NASA Apollo missions and the U.S. Federal Aviation Administration's air traffic control systems.

IBM SYSTEM/360 MODEL 91 CONSOLE,
1968

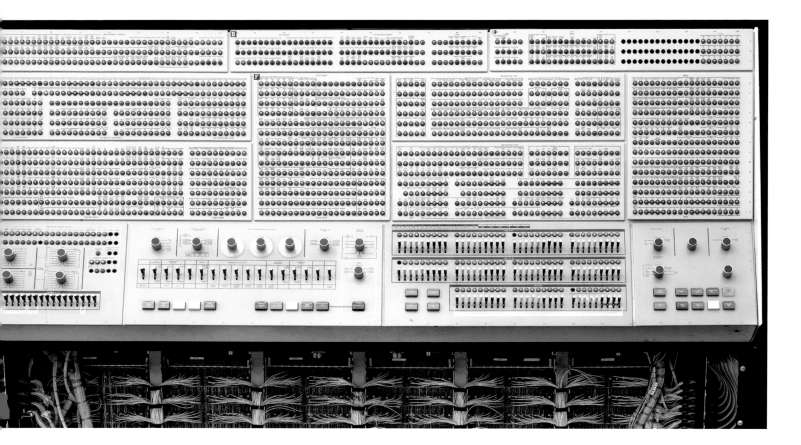

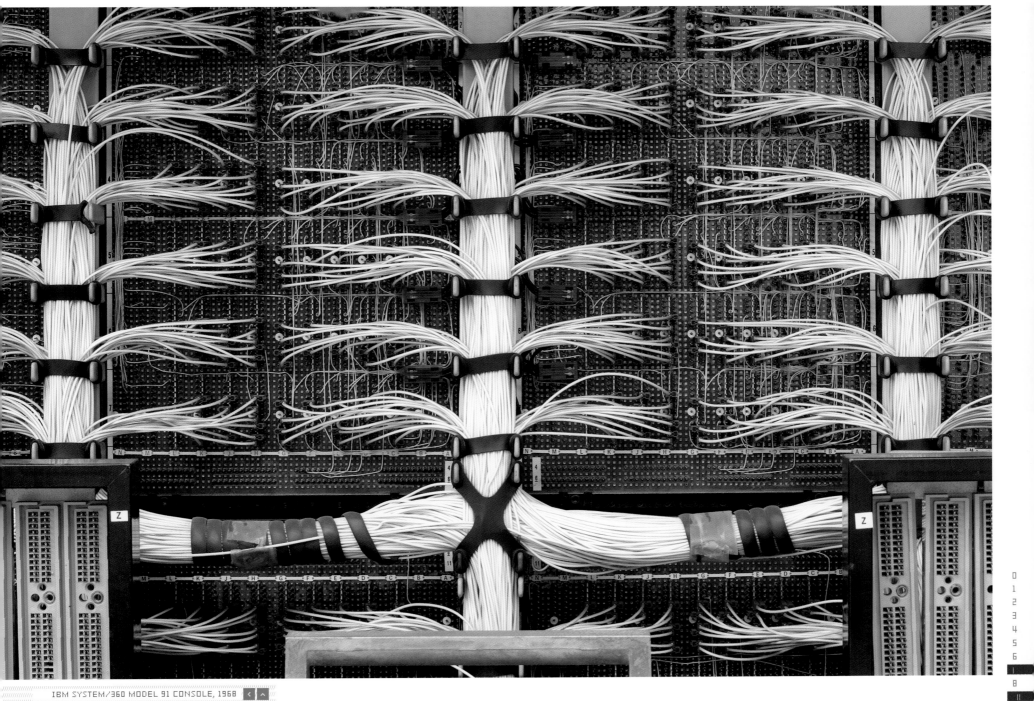

IBM SYSTEM/360 MODEL 91 CONSOLE, 1968

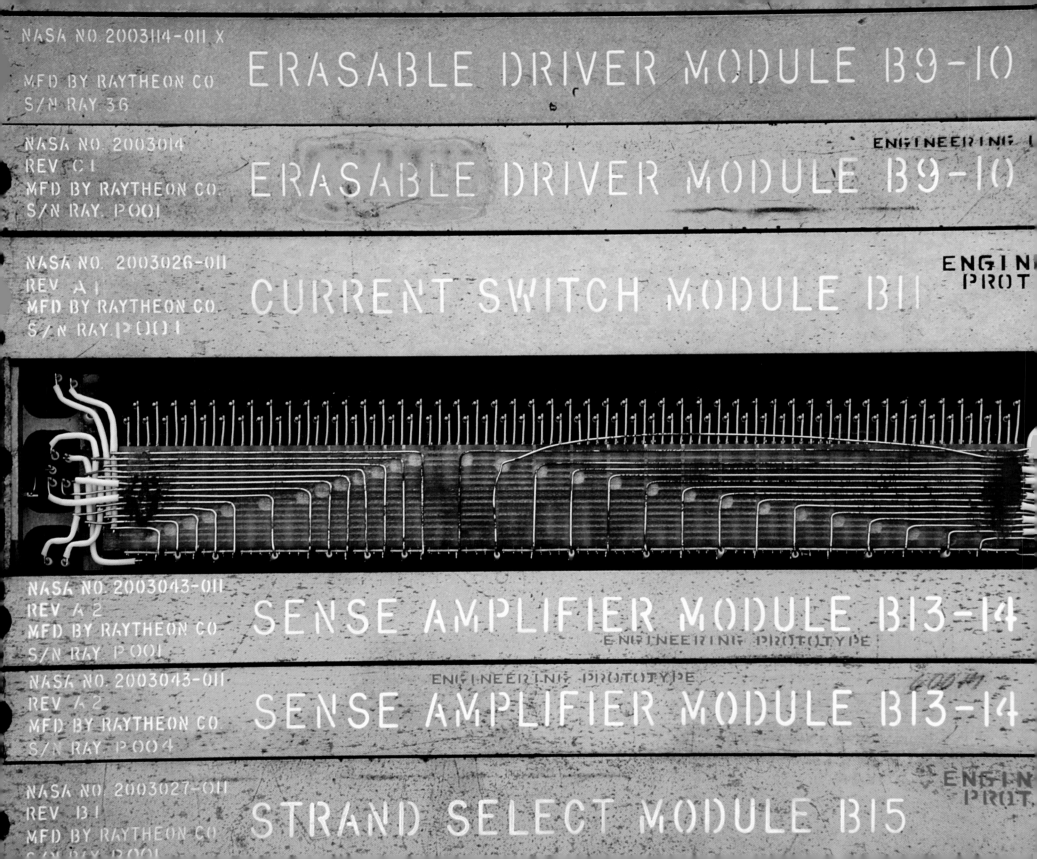

NASA NO. 2003114-011 X
MFD BY RAYTHEON CO
S/N RAY 36

ERASABLE DRIVER MODULE B9-10

NASA NO. 2003014
REV C1
MFD BY RAYTHEON CO.
S/N RAY. POOI

ENGINEERING L

ERASABLE DRIVER MODULE B9-10

NASA NO. 2003026-011
REV A1
MFD BY RAYTHEON CO.
S/N RAY POOI

ENGIN
PROT

CURRENT SWITCH MODULE B11

NASA NO. 2003043-011
REV A2
MFD BY RAYTHEON CO
S/N RAY POOI

SENSE AMPLIFIER MODULE B13-14

ENGINEERING PROTOTYPE

ENGINEERING PROTOTYPE

NASA NO. 2003043-011
REV A2
MFD BY RAYTHEON CO.
S/N RAY POO4

SENSE AMPLIFIER MODULE B13-14

NASA NO. 2003027-011
REV B1
MFD BY RAYTHEON CO
S/N RAY. POOI

ENGIN
PROT

STRAND SELECT MODULE B15

APOLLO GUIDANCE COMPUTER

NAME

YEAR CREATED   1965

CREATOR   MIT/RAYTHEON

COST $250,000

MEMORY   4K RAM, 24K ROM CORE ROPE

..//

Arguably, the modern computer industry was spurred in large part by the cold war, but the space race was another branch, with plenty of cross-pollination. The Apollo Guidance Computer, an embedded system, was developed at the MIT Instrumentation Laboratory and manufactured by Raytheon. Each NASA moon mission used two of them, one for the main command module and one for the lunar module.

The computer used the newly developed integrated circuit, which was small and lightweight. Perhaps to minimize the many variables of space flight, MIT went with just one type of chip, although it used five thousand of them.

Though the embedded computer functioned remarkably well and kept the ships on target and on schedule, when it came to delicate operations, Apollo astronauts wanted to use their own hands for actually landing the lunar module on the moon's surface.

This early, dramatic use of the integrated circuit was important to the development of the semiconductor industry, both for its high profile and its patronage. The interface for the guidance computer was a typical example of the calculator-style layout that would soon be standard in offices around the globe, as the chip would power calculators like the HP-35 by the millions.

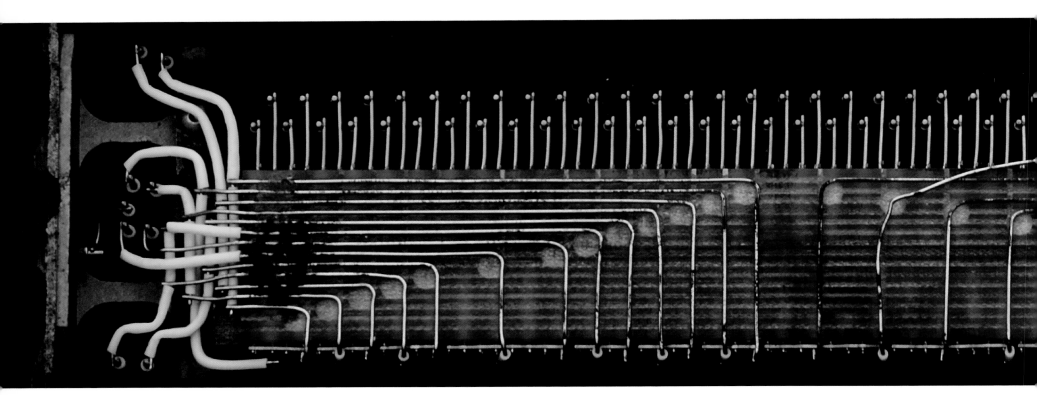

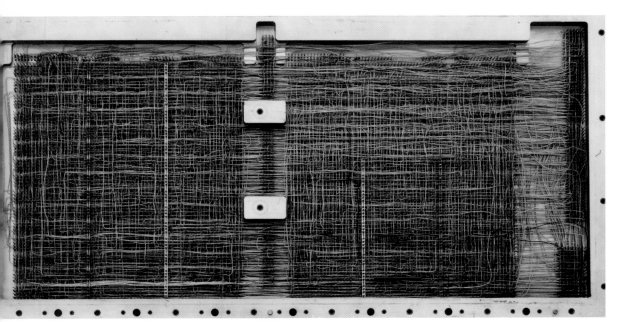

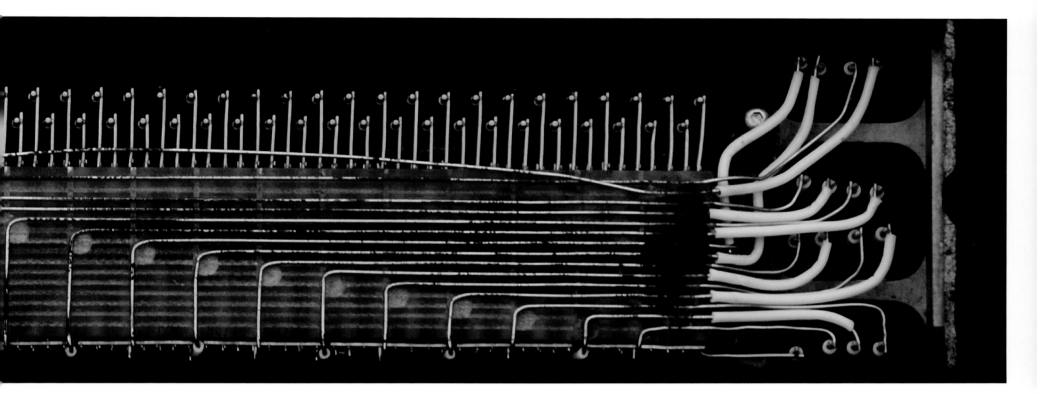

DEC PDP-8

NAME	**DEC PDP-8**
YEAR CREATED	1965
CREATOR	DIGITAL EQUIPMENT CORPORATION
COST	$18,000
MEMORY	4K CORE

..//

Socially provocative and designed with sex appeal, the first minicomputer introduced some themes that have stuck. And it wasn't just the fact that its parent company, DEC, was started with money from proto-venture-capitalist General George F. Doriot. It was the whole business relationship with the customer—a sharing of responsibility and the encouragement to users to educate themselves, which became two of the keynotes of the computer industry. Of course, it helped that DEC's customer base was largely made of engineers.

Years before Apple and GNU/Linux proposed themselves as freedom-loving alternatives to the IBM/Microsoft wall of control, DEC offered a philosophy of computing that stressed sharing. Rather than following what was then the standard IBM practice of leasing a computer as a way of keeping ownership and preventing any modifications, thus keeping programming in the hands of a corporate-sanctioned priestly caste, DEC's PDP (Programmed Data Processor) series, whether by design or from lack of funds, encouraged users to modify, extend, and enhance their machines. DEC engineer Gordon Bell defined the *minicomputer* at the time as the "smallest computer you could build that could do meaningful work," and many PDP-8 computers actually became the sophisticated innards powering stage lighting systems and medical scanners, with users who never had to directly interface with the computer within. The PDP-8 was also very useful for applications like process control in industrial plants, where its small size, low cost, and reliability made it a viable component of manufacturing operations.

Its price, while not cheap by today's standards, allowed universities, schools, and researchers to buy enough models to give their users unprecedented access. In fact, those target markets were necessary, since DEC was counting on sophisticated users to pull much of their own weight. The PDP-8 was one of the first truly "personal" computers whose approachability won the hearts of many young engineers and scientists and turned their minds to computing.

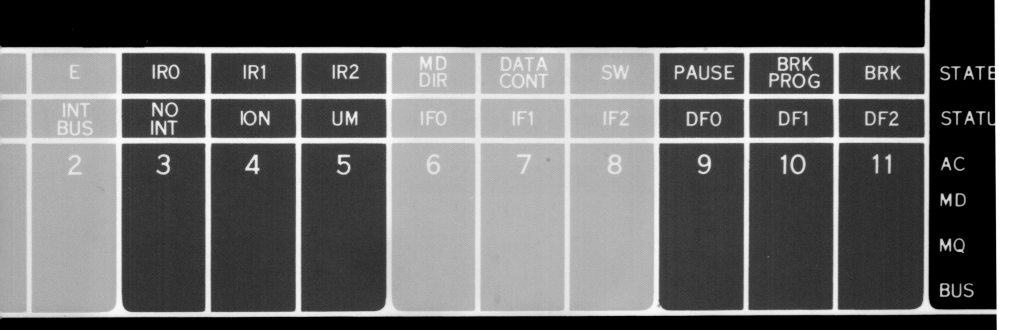

E	IR0	IR1	IR2	MD DIR	DATA CONT	SW	PAUSE	BRK PROG	BRK	STATE
INT BUS	NO INT	ION	UM	IF0	IF1	IF2	DF0	DF1	DF2	STATUS
2	3	4	5	6	7	8	9	10	11	AC
										MD
										MQ
										BUS

| 2 | 3 | 4 | 5 | 6 | 7 | 8 | 9 | 10 | 11 |

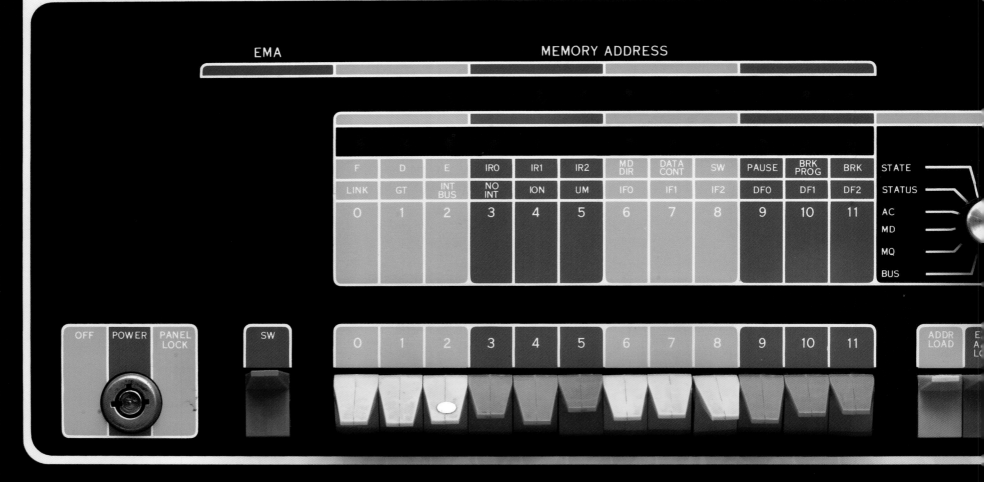

NAME	**DDP-116**
YEAR CREATED	1965
CREATOR	COMPUTER CONTROLS CORPORATION
COST	$28,500
MEMORY	4K CORE

..//

The first 16-bit minicomputer, the DDP-116, was one of a generation of computers that competed with mainframes as the driving force for computing innovation. Unfortunately for the DDP line, its manufacturer, Computer Controls Corporation, was bought by Honeywell—one of the eight major computer manufacturers of the time—which pretty much buried the minicomputer line in favor of established mainframes.

That's not to say that the DDP-116 wasn't successful; it was. But its descendants didn't have nearly the same commercial splash. Its direct successor, however, had a great historical impact: the next-generation DDP-516 became the heart of the Interface Message Processor (or IMP), built by Bolt, Beranek, and Newman, the first device used to connect two computers using packet switching. This would become the ARPANET, the U.S. Defense Department's predecessor of the Internet.

The DDP-116's clean lines and use of white space gave it an especially attractive modernist design, reminiscent to some of a David Hockney California landscape.

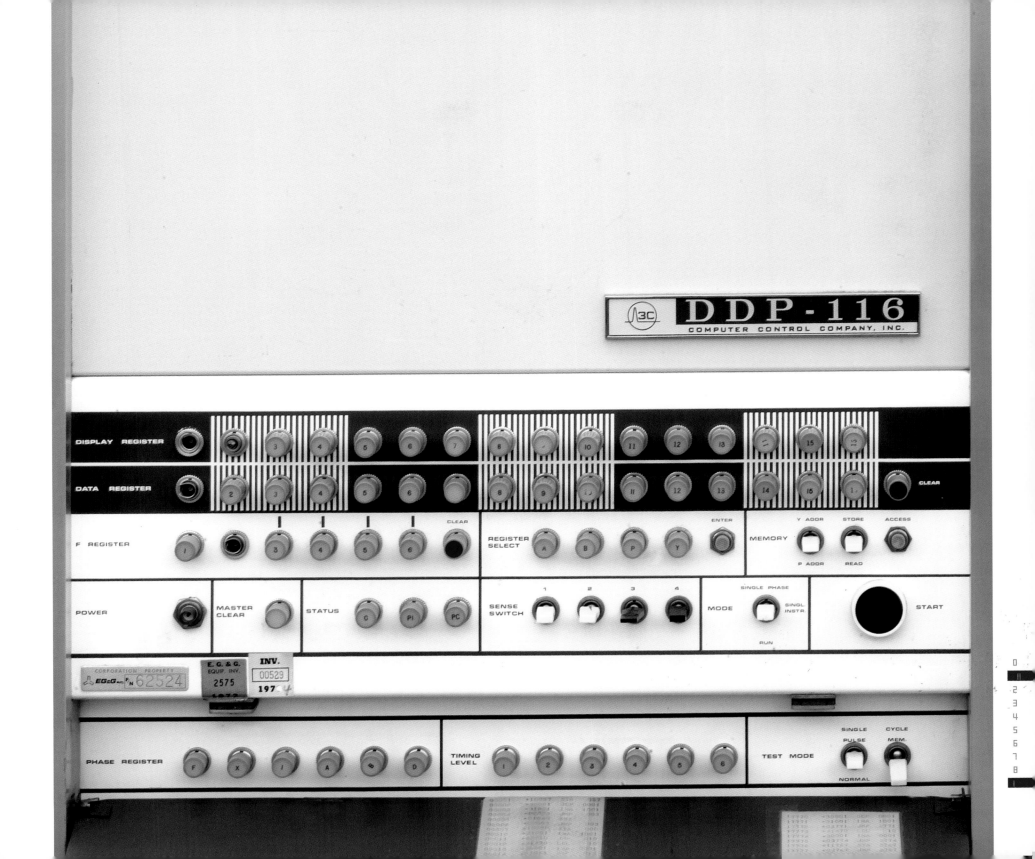

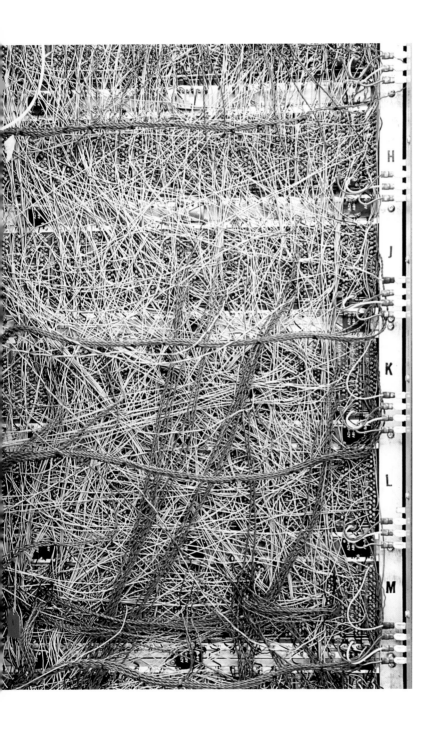

PRIORITY INTERRUPTS

2   3   4   5   6   7   8

INV

PPA
GRD.   1   2   3   4   5   7   8   9   10   11   G
      COLOR DATA IN TO MOTOR   6   AUX AUX
                                       CLK CLK 13   12

PPB
GRD.   G
      SYNCH IN   CELL CLK   DATA SET
                                                       CLK IN

PPC
GRD.   G
      PIL RUN   13   17   14   OUT TO
      PR. OUT   REC   G   PIL 4

PPD
GRD.   SYNC   G
      PIL SYNCH   15   IN   REC SYNC MOTOR RATE
            OUT   TO PIL 6   TO PIL 5

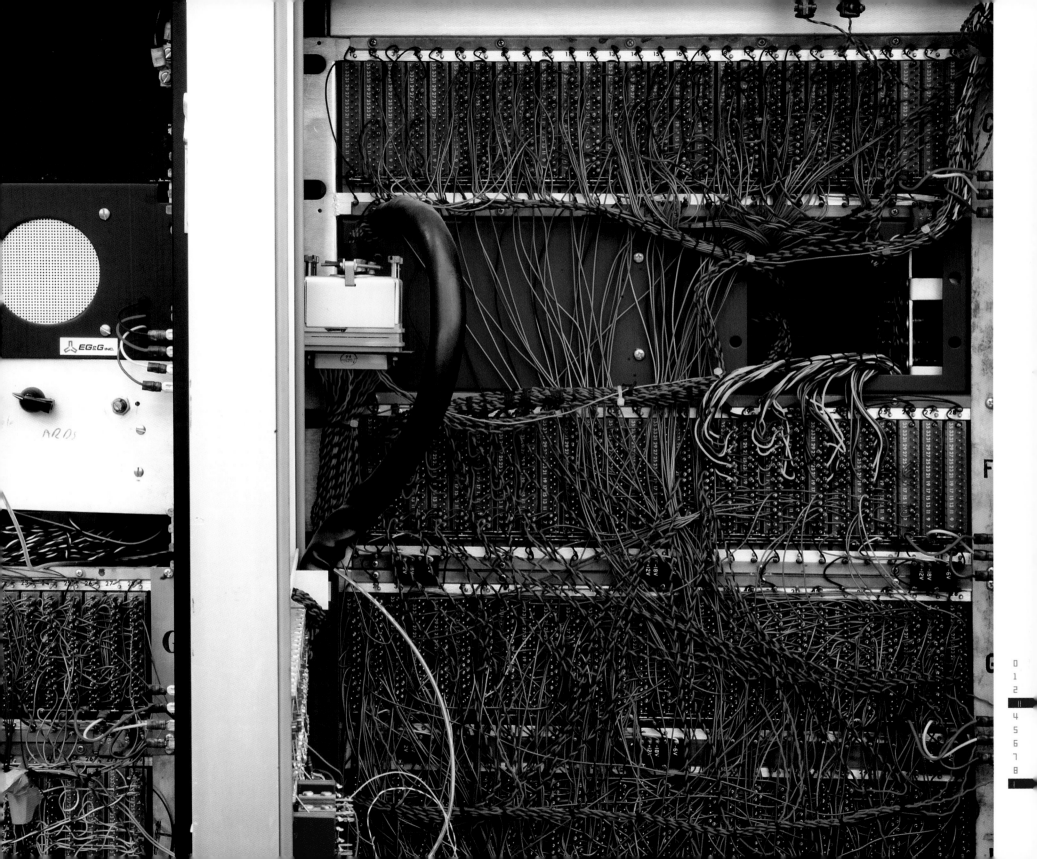

NAME	**CDC 6600**
YEAR CREATED	1964
CREATOR	CONTROL DATA CORPORATION
COST	$7–10 MILLION
MEMORY	64KW + 2MW CORE

../ /

The big eyes are the first thing we notice today, but the CDC 6600 embodied a number of technical firsts in addition to its anthropomorphic face: solid-state design, a very simple architecture, and in general just incredible speed (10 MFLOPS).

The CDC 6600 was engineered by a young Seymour Cray, a man known for the considerable talent he put into making the fastest machines around, and its speed was more a function of Cray's talent for design than of any special hardware. Cray designed computers holistically, not relying simply on lightning-fast processors but making sure the entire design was efficient. Other engineers, such as Gordon Bell, recall being struck by the 6600's elegance. Cray's idea, implemented on the 6600, of multithreaded processors working in parallel, foreshadowed the RISC (Reduced Instruction Set Computing) architecture still popular today.

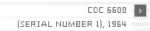

CDC 6600 >
(SERIAL NUMBER 1), 1964

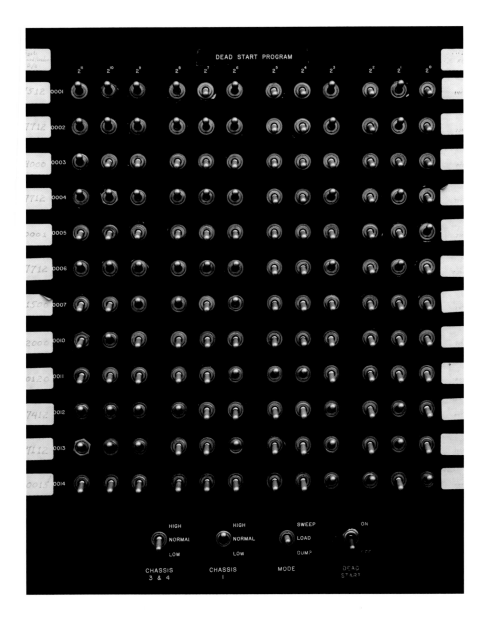

DEAD START PROGRAM

F

G

H

I

J

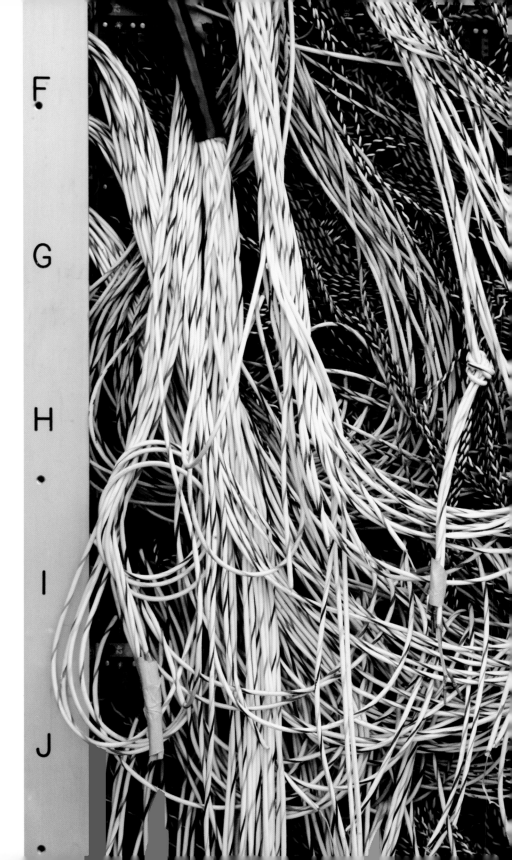

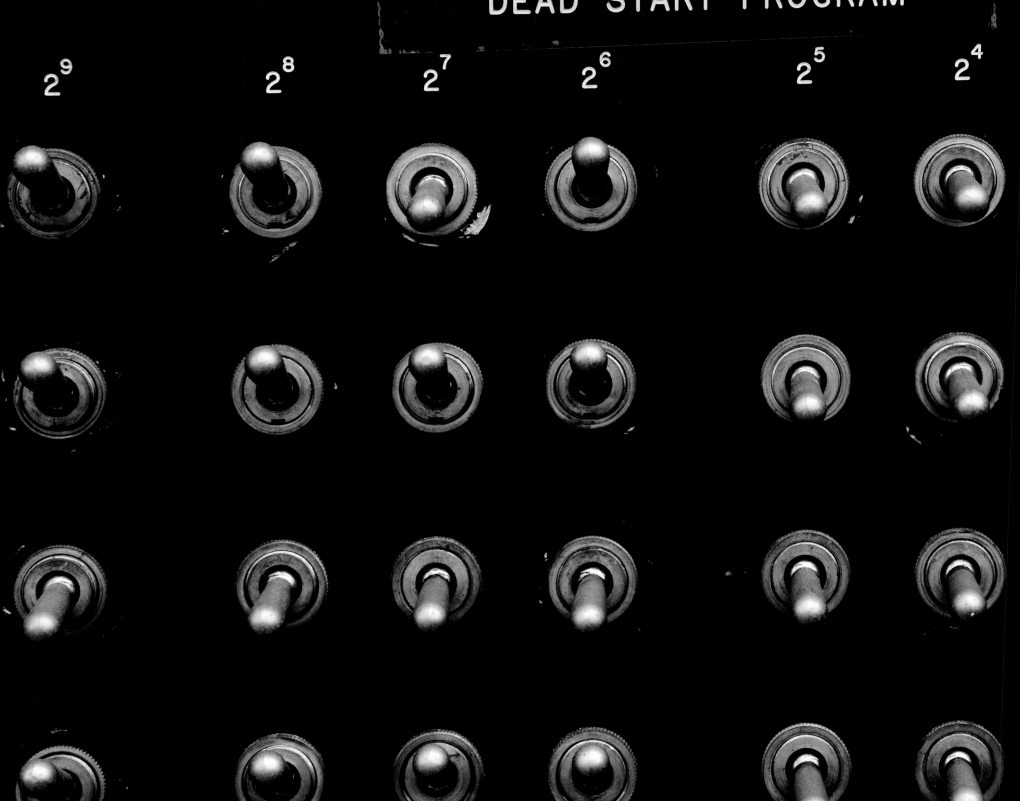

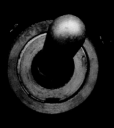

2^3

2^2

The physical design of the 6600 was also groundbreaking, because it cooled the system by pumping Freon through the unit's housing; since very little space was needed for air, connections were shortened and speed was increased. CDC had very good technology and was able to win customers in the scientific and academic worlds, where the customers appreciated the unit's sophisticated design and speed more than they did IBM's slick business sales force.

Most of the 6600s that were produced were sold to nuclear weapons facilities, where the call for such speed was greatest. Amusingly enough, many of the researchers at these facilities passed the time on the 6600 playing computer games, like Spacewars!

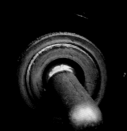

< CDC 6600
(SERIAL NUMBER 1), 1964

0
1
2
3
4
5
6
7
8

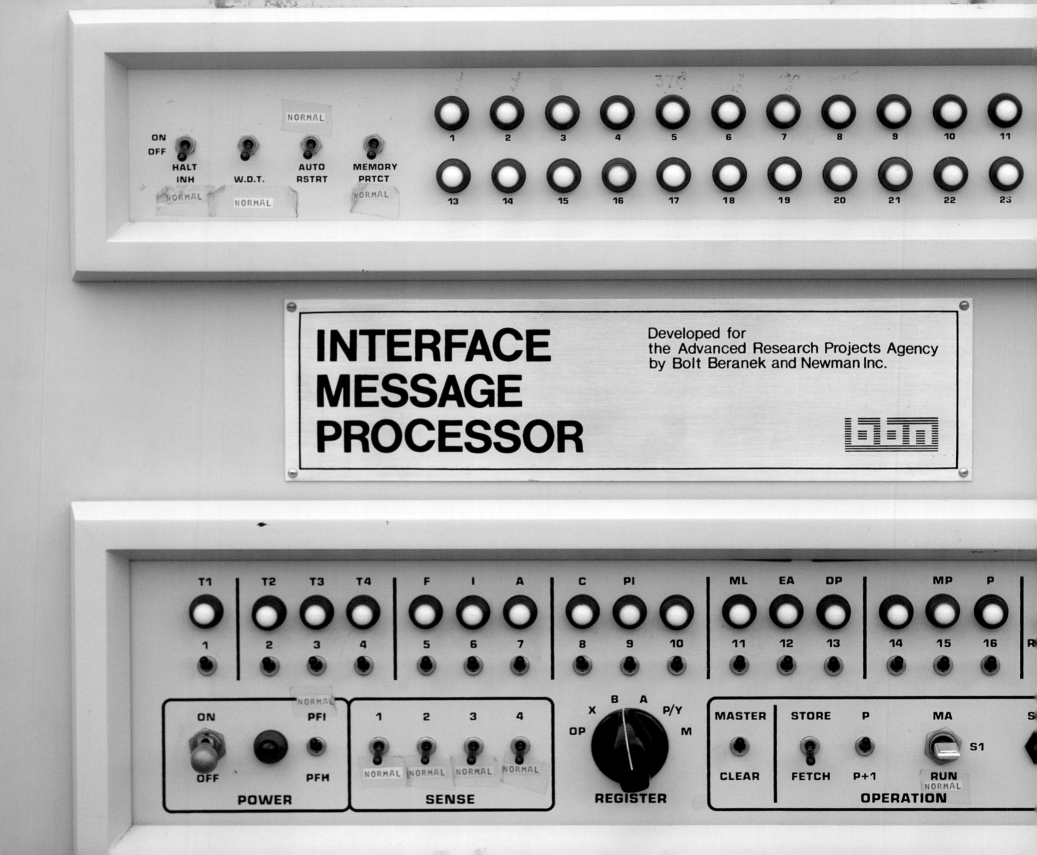

INTERFACE MESSAGE PROCESSOR

Developed for
the Advanced Research Projects Agency
by Bolt Beranek and Newman Inc.

INTERFACE MESSAGE PROCESSOR (IMP)

NAME	
YEAR CREATED	1969
CREATOR	BOLT BERANEK AND NEWMAN (BBN)
COST	$82,200
MEMORY	12KW CORE

The IMP was the first packet router for the ARPANET, the U.S. Defense Department's predecessor of the Internet. DARPA, the Defense Advanced Research Projects Agency, was created to be a driver of new technology, operating independently of the Defense Department's other agencies, all of which were, understandably, concerned with short-term solutions to pressing needs. DARPA's role was to be visionary, and ARPANET was a vision of a world of connected computers whose distribution would allow the network to survive the loss of nodes due to catastrophic failure — often imagined as a nuclear strike.

The ARPANET drew on the work of several independent researchers but was based fundamentally on the ideas of J. C. R. Licklider, who was briefly a DARPA researcher. Licklider envisioned a giant "galactic network" (his phrase) connecting the world, as well as the more prosaic concept of sharing computing resources. Bolt Beranek and Newman, where Licklider worked before joining DARPA, was given the task of building the machine to implement packet switching, in which routers are able to facilitate communication between many nodes simultaneously by splitting up their content into "packets" that find the best route, then reassembling them at the destination. The machine BBN built was driven by a Honeywell 516 minicomputer, efficiently running on only six thousand words of software. The IMP was hooked to a host computer and then connected via modem to a leased line.

Central to the workings of the Internet, then and now, is the ability of distant computers to send "packets" of information to one another. Packet switching was an important development that replaced the traditional circuit switching, which relied on a single dedicated connection and could lead to network outages if one site was taken out. Because computers were often unreliable and used for various tasks, the IMP, essentially a specialized minicomputer, was invented as the ARPANET's information delivery mechanism—each IMP would "store and forward" what it was sent. By making standardized IMPs, a reliable network was built. IMP error checking would confirm that each packet was received at each point along the path and would re-route the message if a particular node was malfunctioning.

"The thing that makes the computer communication network special," Licklider said, "is that it puts the workers, the team members who are geographically distributed, in touch not only with one another, but with the information base with which they work all the time, so that when they get to developing plans, the blueprints don't have to be copied and sent all around the country—the blueprints come out of the database and appear on everybody's scopes. The correlation, or the coordination of the activity, is essentially right there in the computer network itself. This is obviously going to make a tremendous difference in how we plan, organize, and execute almost anything of any intellectual consequence."

This particular machine was number ten in the network.

INTERFACE MESSAGE
PROCESSOR (IMP), 1969

NAME	**KITCHEN COMPUTER (HONEYWELL H316 MINICOMPUTER)**
YEAR CREATED	1969
CREATOR	HONEYWELL (FOR NEIMAN MARCUS)
COST	$10,600
MEMORY	4KW CORE

..//

KITCHEN >
COMPUTER
(HONEYWELL
H316
PEDESTAL
MOUNT), 1969

"If she can only cook as well as Honeywell can compute," ran the headline advertising this item in the Neiman Marcus catalog. Imagine the housewife—or, more likely, the kitchen staff, given the genteel audience of the Neiman Marcus catalog—staring dumbstruck at the arrival of this beast into her cooking space. It was certainly modish and came fully stocked with a Honeywell 316 minicomputer inside, and it was accompanied by a two-week programming course. But its usability was laughable.

Despite some thought having gone into the facade, the interface was simply lights and switches—good for setting the mood for a *Lost in Space*-style TV dinner, but not for a new-bie programmer or cook. (Come to think of it, a TV dinner wouldn't require a computer to fetch the recipe.) For only ten thousand dollars, you could have a table that wasn't quite flat.

It's unclear why none of them sold.

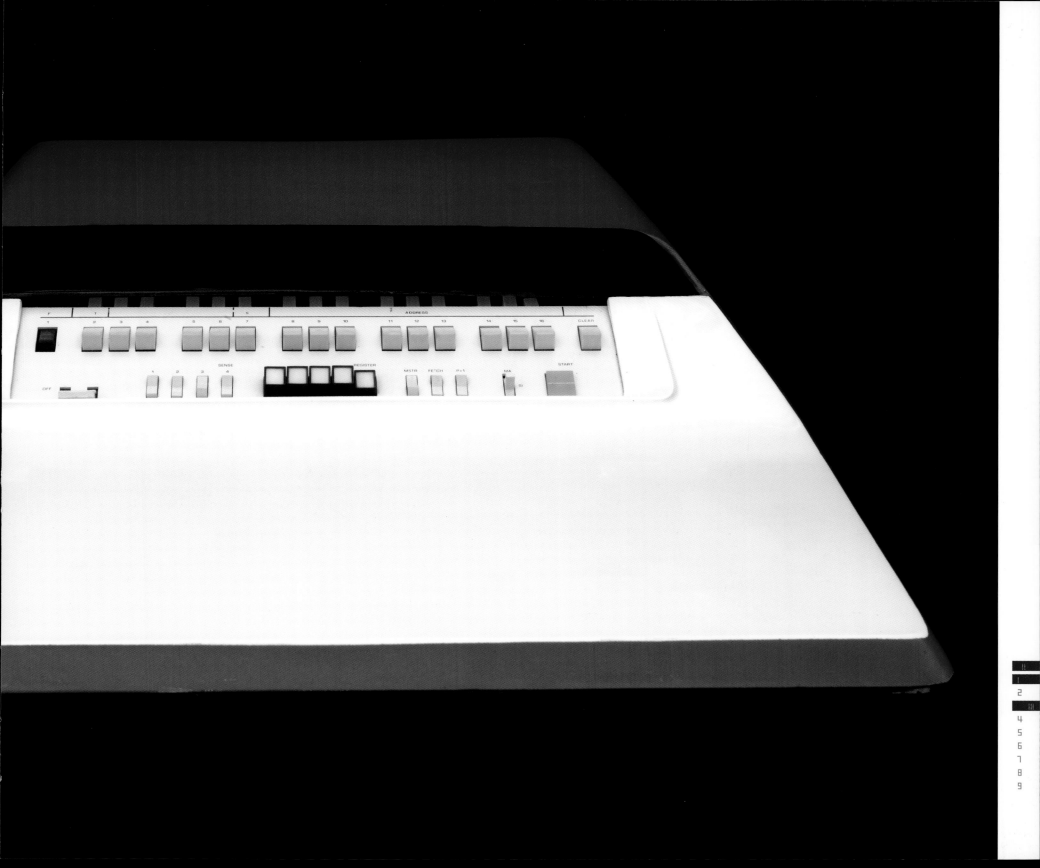

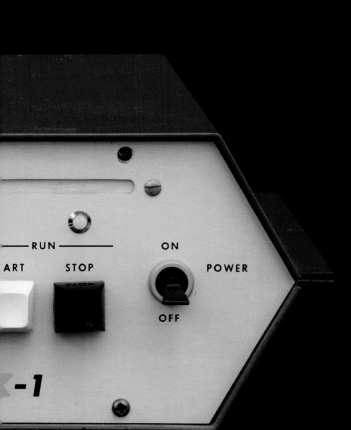

NAME	**KENBAK-1**
YEAR CREATED	1971
CREATOR	KENBAK CORPORATION
COST	$750
MEMORY	256 BYTES SEMICONDUCTOR
PROCESSOR	TTL (TRANSISTOR-TRANSISTOR LOGIC)

The first personal computer was sold as a kit, but unfortunately, not many sold. John V. Blankenbaker advertised his creation, the Kenbak-1, in the September 1971 issue of *Scientific American*, offering it at a rather high price, considering its limitations once assembled. The machine did not have a microprocessor, input and output were limited to a set of switches and lights, and with 256 bytes, there wasn't a whole lot a user could do.

Nonetheless, education was the main point, and according to the advertisement, "the easy-to-understand manuals assume the reader is approaching a computer for the first time." It's not surprising that not too many institutions bought Blankenbaker's kit, but it was a good try. Only forty or so of the squashed blue hexagonal computers were made, and the company closed in 1973.

KENBAK-1, 1971

NAME	# HP-35
YEAR CREATED	1972
CREATOR	HEWLETT-PACKARD COMPANY
COST	$395
PROCESSOR	CUSTOM 56-BIT SERIAL

..//

It's easy to forget the history of calculators, and the great contribution they have made. The first computers were, of course, calculators, and later innovations were built on the reliability of earlier generations of adding machines. The creation of the integrated circuit made possible the shrinking of processing power to the extent that a handheld unit could do calculations previously thought miraculous when performed by room-size machines costing millions of dollars.

Perhaps it was because the slide rule was as common to engineers as ties are to bankers, but Hewlett-Packard cofounder Bill Hewlett had a vision—in contradiction to market research—that a shirt-pocket-size calculator would be a hit. Of course, he was right: Hewlett and his colleagues, as much as anyone, fit the model for a target audience and proved that Hewlett's gut instinct was as valuable as market research.

The care that went into the design of the HP-35 was also remarkable; Hewlett considered which keys would be most often used, and he made those more prominent by virtue of color. Users appreciated the thoughtful design and foresight, and the calculator beat all sales estimates despite its use of the advantageous, but arcane, "Reverse Polish Notation" to enter information.

Two years later, the programmable HP-65 model was introduced and marketed as a "personal computer." Sadly for HP, the same vision didn't hold when a young employee named Steve Wozniak proposed that Hewlett-Packard create an actual personal computer: HP rejected his design, and he quit the company over that and went on to co-found Apple Computer.

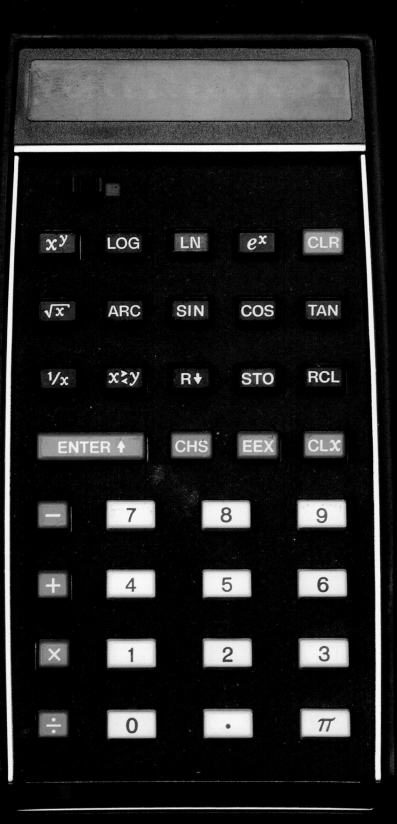

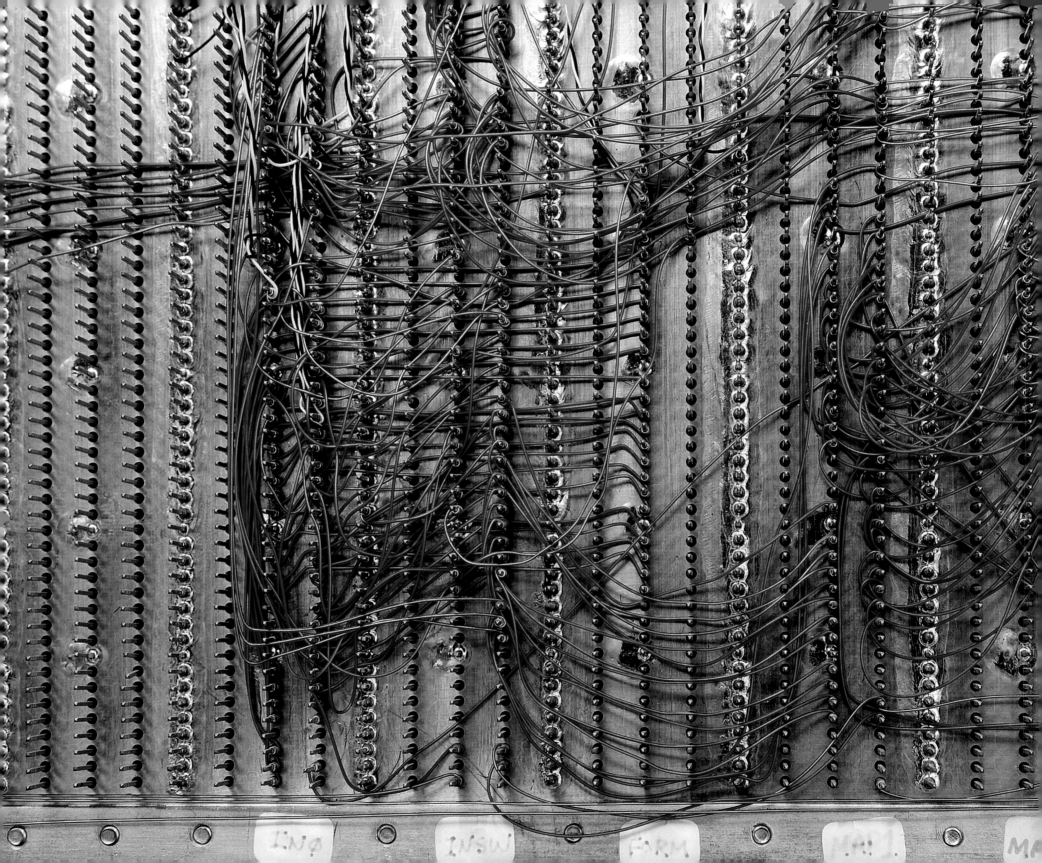

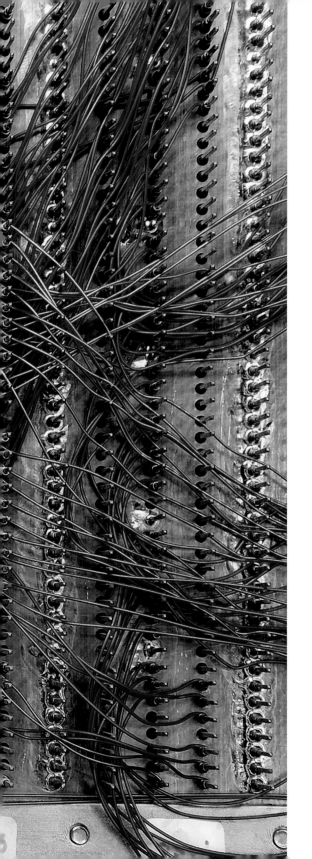

SUPERPAINT

NAME	SUPERPAINT
YEAR CREATED	1973
CREATOR	XEROX PARC, DICK SHOUP
COST	NOT FOR SALE
MEMORY	2K BIT FRAME BUFFER MEMORY

The progenitor of all today's paint programs (as well as other pixel manipulators, such as Photoshop) was designed mostly using a pencil. Built by Dick Shoup, this combination software-hardware video graphics system, which utilized an eight-bit-per-pixel frame buffer, was a product of the innovation vortex that was Xerox PARC in the 1970s.

Most modern computer systems contain a fair a bit of DNA from SuperPaint—and it doesn't usually take too long to find. The interface featured the now familiar concept of a palette of tools and colors to be picked by the user. If the user didn't wish to use the palette of tools to draw, or "videopaint," as Shoup called it, a video camera could be attached and used to import images directly. SuperPaint pointed toward a future of color interfaces at a time when most were monochrome or grayscale, and its picture resolution of 480 by 640 pixels was nothing to sneeze at.

Besides being a tool for creating still images, SuperPaint was also a distinguished animation machine (as well as an example of the computer world's love of crafting names by smashing two words into one). Notable works created using Shoup's machine include the title graphics for *Over Easy*, a PBS series produced by KQED in San Francisco in 1977, and aids for visualizing scientific experiments and spacecraft movement at NASA for the Pioneer Venus mission in 1978. Through these achievements, SuperPaint had the rare distinction of winning Shoup and Xerox an Emmy award in 1983, and Shoup and his collaborators Alvy Ray Smith and Tom Porter an Academy Award in 1998 for technical innovations in developing paint systems.

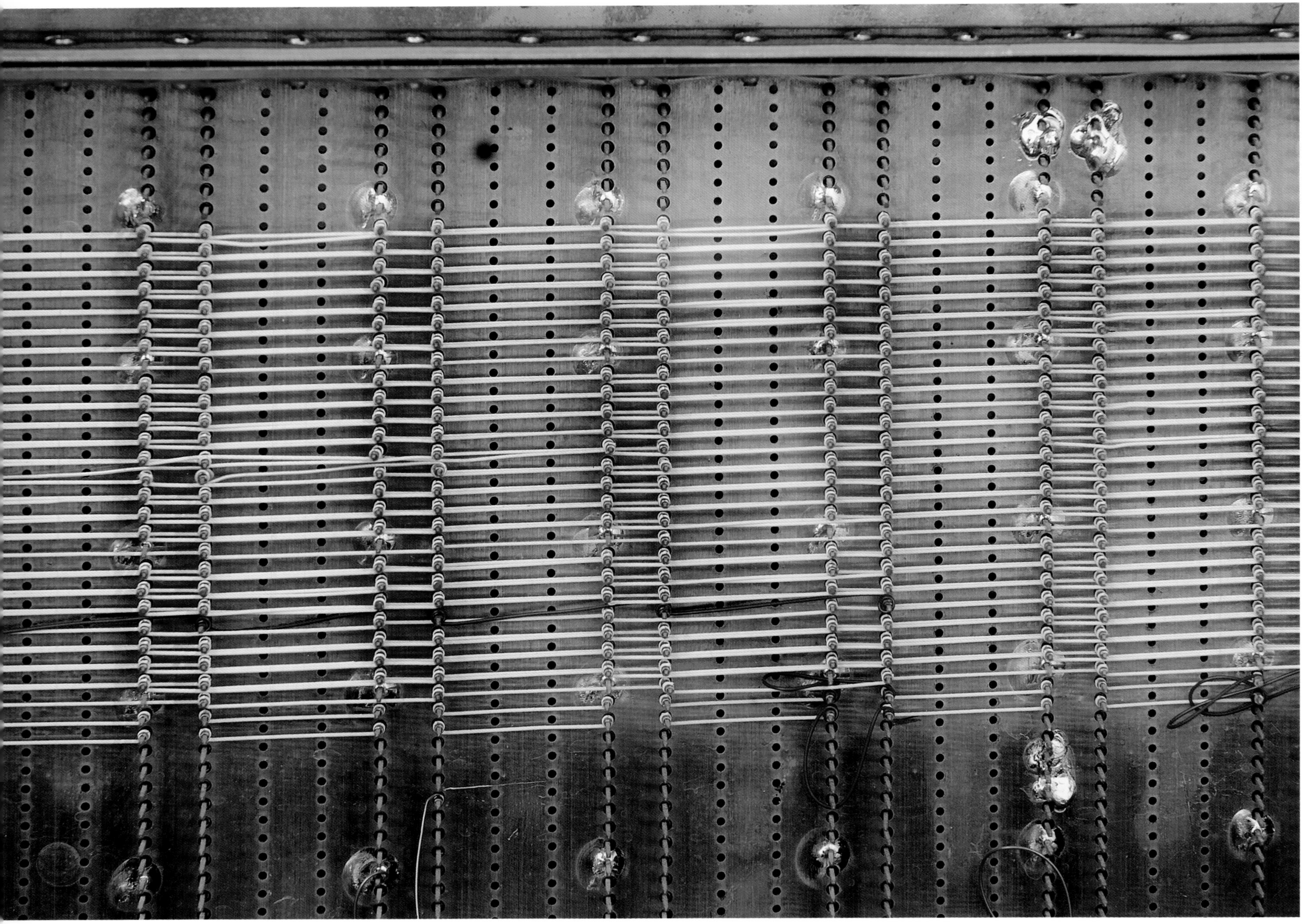

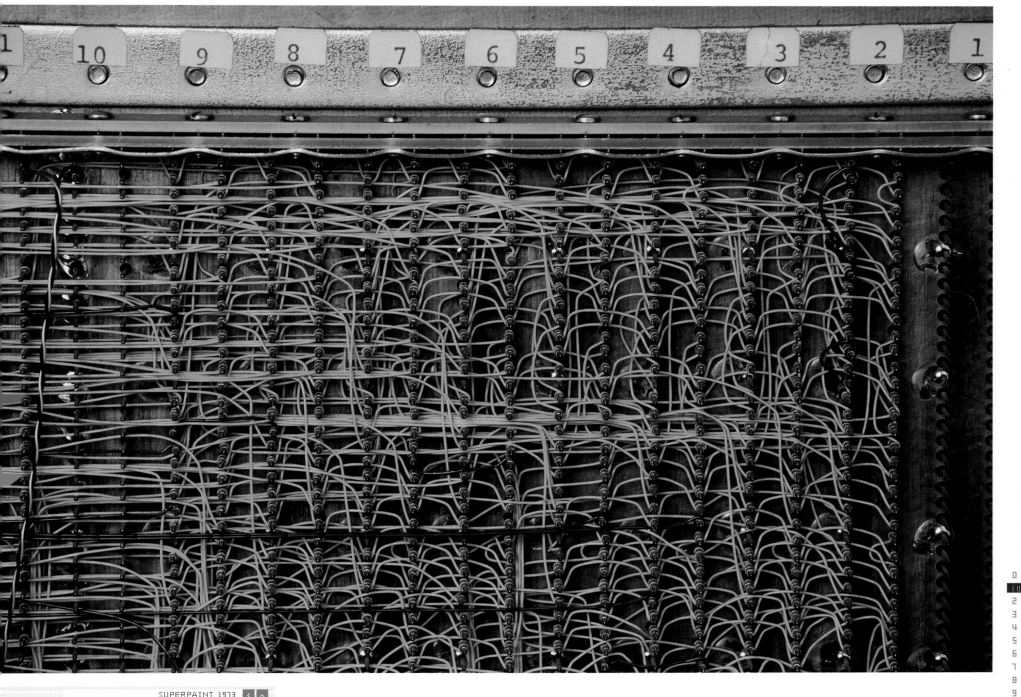

SUPERPAINT, 1973

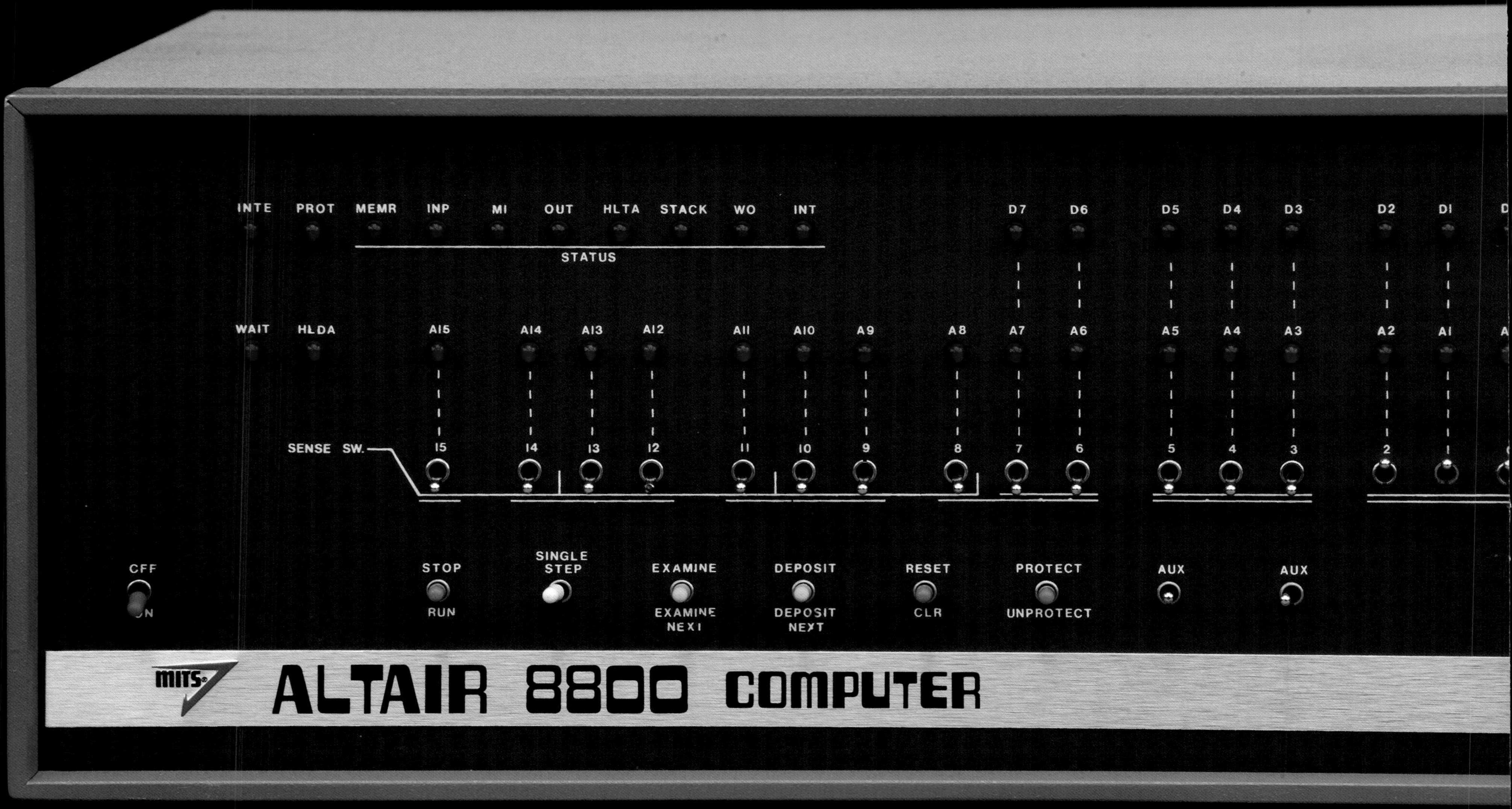
INTE PROT MEMR INP MI OUT HLTA STACK WO INT
STATUS
D7 D6 D5 D4 D3 D2 DI
WAIT HLDA
AI5 AI4 AI3 AI2 AII AI0 A9 A8 A7 A6 A5 A4 A3 A2 AI
SENSE SW.
I5 I4 I3 I2 II I0 9 8 7 6 5 4 3 2
OFF
ON
STOP
RUN
SINGLE STEP
EXAMINE
EXAMINE NEXT
DEPOSIT
DEPOSIT NEXT
RESET
CLR
PROTECT
UNPROTECT
AUX
AUX
MITS
ALTAIR 8800 COMPUTER

NAME	# ALTAIR 8800
YEAR CREATED	1975
CREATOR	MICRO INSTRUMENTATION AND TELEMETRY SYSTEMS (MITS)
PRICE	$397
MEMORY	256 BYTES SEMICONDUCTOR
PROCESSOR	INTEL 8080

..//

It's 1975 and you really want your own computer. Maybe you and your colleagues call your-selves "hobbyists" and work as programmers on a mainframe or other computer, with usage doled out by the bureaucrats running the place. Spurred on by a cover story in *Popular Electronics* magazine, you plunk down a hefty amount and in return receive a kit for a far-out-looking blue box, apparently named after a destination in a *Star Trek* episode. It sounded cool, but after you assembled the pricey circuitry, what could the Altair 8800 do?

The answer is, not much; at least when it first shipped, when the most you could do, unless you happened to own a paper-tape reader, was enter a program by flipping switches and hope to get some blinking lights in reply. Owning an Altair 8800 required not only a lot of vision, but a lot of patience as well.

The force behind this personal computer was Ed Roberts, a former U.S. Air Force officer who mixed a dictatorial style with a near-obsession involving the technologies he was developing. Roberts had his faults, but his vision for marketing computers to the newly growing community of hobbyists was timely. Later, when Roberts added a (remarkably unreliable) memory board, it became feasible to run a higher-level programming lan-guage, BASIC, with enough memory to actually accomplish something.

This programming language, Altair BASIC, was written by Bill Gates and Paul Allen in a one-month period, and was actually very popular with hobbyists, but the memory boards needed to run it were earning disdain. Soon competitors began marketing better boards. As a way of retaining customers, MITS offered a discount on BASIC when it was bundled with the board—but left it overpriced on its own. Customers balked and began making unapproved paper tape copies of BASIC. Gates was incensed, and he penned his famous anti-copying screed, "An Open Letter to Hobbyists," a line in the sand that met with mixed results.

NAME	ILLIAC IV
YEAR CREATED	1975
CREATOR	UNIVERSITY OF ILLINOIS AND BURROUGHS CORPORATION
PRICE	$31 MILLION
MEMORY	16MW

..//

Nearly ten years in development, this Burroughs supercomputer was a test bed created as its developers attempted to craft a speedier way to handle computing tasks known as single instruction, multiple data (SIMD). Funded by DARPA, the Defense Advanced Research Projects Agency, this costly system never quite lived up to its promise or expense, but it inspired researchers of parallel processing (and attracted the attention of antiestablishment student protesters).

The main idea behind the ILLIAC IV's SIMD model was that it would split a problem up so that many processing elements could execute the same instruction on different data. Although it was tricky to come up with problems that could be expressed this way, this system was very efficient at solving such problems when they could be found. For a while it was the fastest computer in the world, as long as it was doing a task that was designed to be solved in parallel.

As protests against the war in Vietnam generalized into attacks on the "military-industrial complex," the safety of the ILLIAC project on the University of Illinois campus came into question. After activists in 1970 called for a day of "Illiaction" and wanted to shut down the project, largely because of its military associations, the researchers and equipment were moved to NASA's secure Ames Research Center in Mountain View, California. But the project never regained momentum, and in the end only 64 processing elements were built, out of an original 256 for which the computer was designed. It was decommissioned in 1982.

NAME	**CRAY-1**
YEAR CREATED	1976
CREATOR	CRAY RESEARCH, INC.
COST	$5 MILLION TO $10 MILLION
MEMORY	4MW SEMICONDUCTOR
SPEED	160 MFLOPS

NAME	**CRAY-2**
YEAR CREATED	1985
CREATOR	CRAY RESEARCH, INC.
COST	$12 MILLION TO $20 MILLION
MEMORY	UP TO 512MW SEMICONDUCTOR
SPEED	488 MFLOPS/CPU (UP TO 8 CPUS)

< CRAY-2, 1985

NAME	**CRAY-3**
YEAR CREATED	1993
CREATOR	CRAY COMPUTER CORPORATION
COST	$30 MILLION
MEMORY	2GW SEMICONDUCTOR
SPEED	15 GFLOPS

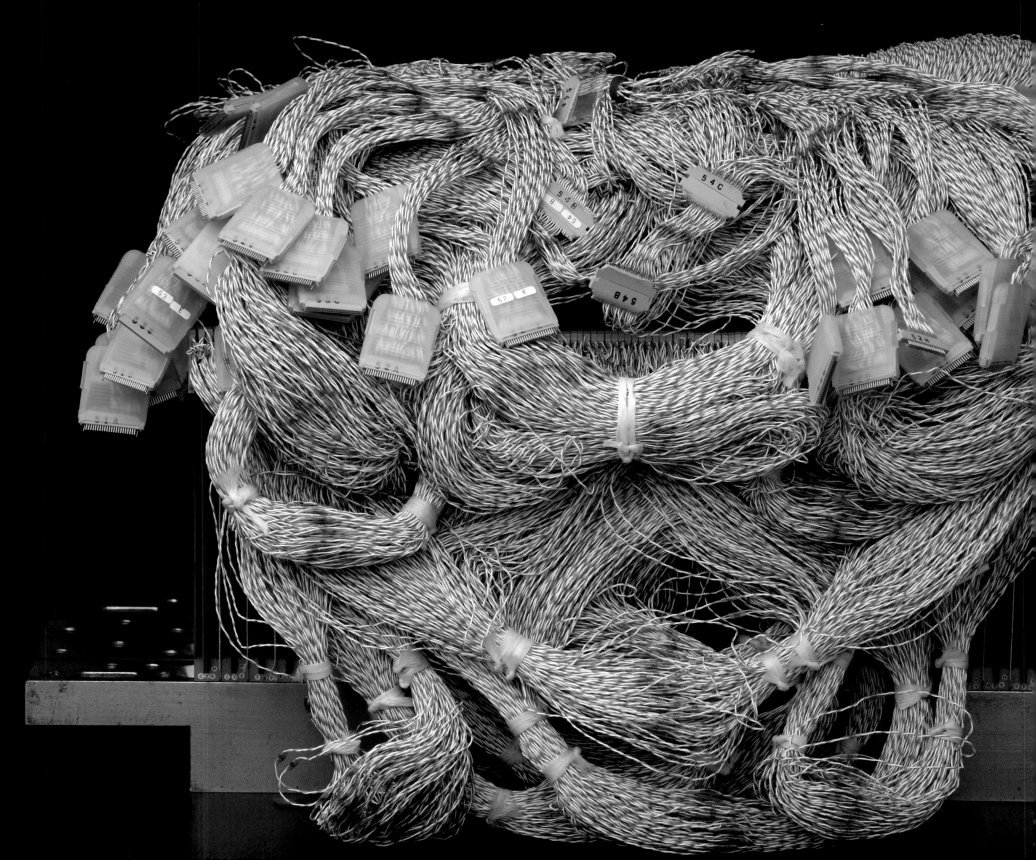

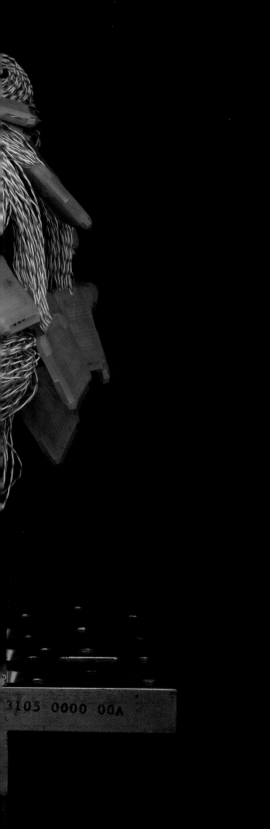

.://

Building supercomputers was a dream, an aspiration, and a life's pursuit for Seymour Cray, and his work on the computers that bore his name was the culmination of work he had done for the U.S. Navy, for CDC, and finally for his namesake company. When Cray left CDC in 1972, after his work on the 6600, 7600, and minimally the 8600, he took much of the supercomputer fire with him.

While Cray's departure from CDC wasn't overly dramatic, his impact on supercomputing was. Cray artfully designed computers so that each part worked to efficiently speed up the whole, and he usually didn't rely on the newest experimental components, preferring instead to tweak existing technologies for maximum performance. For instance, the Cray-1 was the first Cray machine to use integrated circuits, despite their having been on the market for about a decade. At 160 MFLOPS, the Cray-1 was the fastest machine at the time, and despite what seemed like only a niche market for expensive superfast machines, Cray Research sold more than a hundred of them.

Form and size were always concerns for Cray, as far back as his days developing the CDC 160, which was built into an ordinary desk. There was also a big concern with the heat that could be generated by so many parts being packaged so tightly together, so Cray's designs typically involved unique cooling solutions, whether it be Freon on the Cray-1, or Fluorinert, in which the Cray-2's circuit boards were immersed. In fact, the Cray-2 was smaller and twelve times faster than the Cray-1, available with up to eight processors.

The Cray-3 was a departure from the Cray standard of cleverly using fairly mundane parts and represented the first use of gallium arsenide semiconductors instead of the much more familiar (and much cheaper) silicon. Seymour Cray left Cray research and founded the Cray Computer Corporation to develop the Cray-3 when the old company declared the new computer a low priority. But it wasn't company politics that did in the Cray-3; it was international politics, as the end of the cold war meant fewer perceived uses for supercomputers.

CRAY-3, 1993

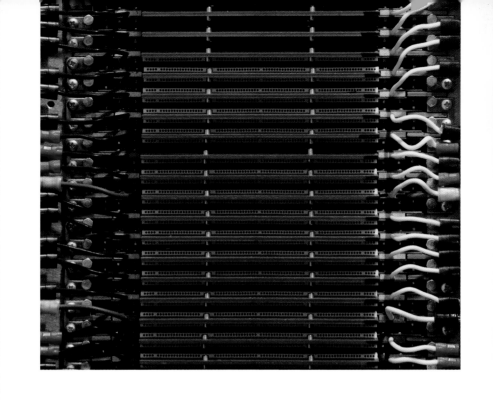

CRAY-3, 1993

NAME	**APPLE I**
YEAR CREATED	1976
CREATOR	APPLE COMPUTER COMPANY
PRICE	$666.66
MEMORY	4KB SEMICONDUCTOR
PROCESSOR	MOS TECHNOLOGY 6502

..//

Of course people would want their own computer. But when Steve Wozniak offered a design for one to his employer, Hewlett-Packard, it was rejected. With fate on his side, Wozniak introduced the Apple I to Silicon Valley's Homebrew Computer Club, even if it was little more than a kit. Kits were popular with hobbyists, and the offerings were often crafted by users onto wooden boards, as pictured here.

Sensing that the market for a personal computer went beyond people who had the time to put together their own, Wozniak (or "Woz" as he is known, and evidently signs his name) and his friend Steve Jobs sold fifty pre-built Apple I computers to The Byte Shop in Mountain View. If the biblical allusions of the price and the image of temptation represented by an apple weren't enough, many believed that "Apple" was a reference to the

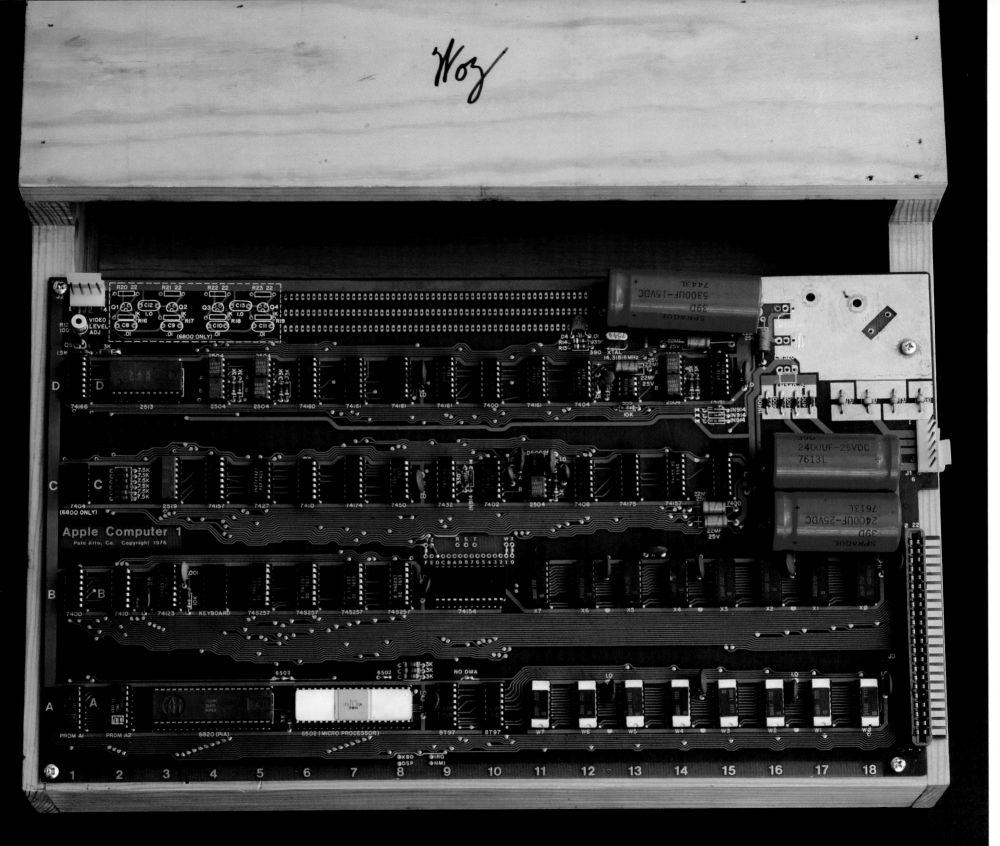

Beatles' Apple Corps record label. All of these cultural markers conveyed that this computer, and the company that made it, was for cool people who were in on the joke and ready to take the reins of technological power—or at least have a bit more fun with it. The computer industry was beginning to make serious inroads into popular culture—or was it the reverse? It was Steve Jobs whose crafty marketing sense pushed all of these themes into play. Not coincidentally, the idea of the computer "evangelist" proselytizing about new hard- or software took hold at Apple.

About two hundred models of the Apple I were sold—not as many as the Altair, but to Jobs and Wozniak, they established the concept and provided the fuel to form a company to launch the Apple II, a runaway success. And some important lessons were learned: Maybe it was the lack of a case that impressed on Jobs the importance of a good-looking box. Either way, no one has done more than Apple to turn the home-brewed computer into beautiful, consumer-friendly machines, from the Macintosh to the iPod.

NAME	**APPLE II**
YEAR CREATED	1977
CREATOR	APPLE COMPUTER, INC.
COST	$1,298 WITH 4KB OF RAM; $2,638 WITH 48KB OF RAM
MEMORY	4K SEMICONDUCTOR
PROCESSOR	MOS TECHNOLOGY 6502

..//

Spurred on by the small but encouraging success of the original Apple, the two Steves, Wozniak and Jobs, retreated to the garage (Jobs's) to craft the personal computer that was the most convincing case yet that such an item could have a mass market. The Apple II started where the Apple I left off, namely, with a case. It didn't look like an object dropped from a starship or developed in a military lab. It had the familiar, prosaic form of an elongated beige typewriter, though additions like the television monitor and the cassette player used to store programs made it look a little like a college-dorm entertainment center.

If its appearance was familiar, the Apple II was also attractive to consumers in a way that previous computers just weren't—even if their manufacturers tried. It shipped with high-resolution color graphics and sound, and it had a rainbow-colored apple logo that seemed both fresh and optimistic. Said Wozniak, "The Apple II, more than any other early machine, made *computer* a word that could be said in homes. It presented a computer concept that included fun and games—human-type things." The ability to have a business and a social side was an important sign of computing's growing relevance.

The price made the Apple II affordable for businesspeople, well-off families, and schools. It was in the education sector that its influence lasted longest—although it certainly made its mark on business as the first platform to run VisiCalc, the first consumer spreadsheet program. It was the programs that really hooked people, and the Apple II had a great roster of educational and entertainment software. By attracting developers, a snowball effect occurred, and a new generation of developers became attracted and then obsessed.

TRS-80 MODEL 1 (AND MODEL 100)

NAME	
YEAR CREATED	1977
CREATOR	TANDY CORPORATION
COST	$399 ($599 WITH MONITOR)
MEMORY	4KB ROM
PROCESSOR	Z-80

Despite Apple's marketing message of personal empowerment and freedom, they weren't giving away those Apple IIs. A computer—especially one with a price tag of $1,300 or more—was beyond the comfort range of most people in the country, and few parents considered such a thing necessary to child development. As far as business went, it would be a while before a "killer app"—a must-have application—would be developed for machines available at an affordable price.

The TRS-80 was in part an antidote to this. If parents were convinced of a computer's necessity, but their pocketbooks couldn't support an Apple, then $399, or even $599, was worth considering. For a business that wanted to experiment with computing, that was a reasonable asking price.

The system was developed by the Tandy buyer Don French and Homebrew Computer Club leader Steve Leininger, who was quoted by *Creative Computing* magazine at the time as saying he had rejected a company plan to sell a computer kit because "too many people can't solder." This was an interesting admission from the company that owned Radio Shack, famous at that time for selling electronics parts to hobbyists. Nevertheless, the TRS-80 was actually rather sophisticated. Four kilobytes of RAM were matched with 4K of ROM holding Radio Shack's proprietary version of BASIC. The silver-and-black color scheme—even more than a beige box—evoked a kind of futuristic proletarian chic. Like other, similar systems, the TRS-80 used a cassette tape player as a storage device.

The early portable TRS-80 Model 100, designed by Kyocera and released in 1983, was evidence that, by that time, beige was winning the color war. Rugged and able to start up immediately, the Model 100 was utilitarian and much-beloved by traveling reporters.

NAME	# MINITEL
YEAR CREATED	1981 (THIS MODEL)
CREATOR	FRANCE TELECOM/ALCATEL
COST	FREE TO FRENCH CITIZENS

../ /

As the Web was being developed in the early 1990s at the nuclear research institute CERN, in Switzerland and France there was already a well-established French network of millions of users of Minitel, a system that combined terminals with a closed network that let users do many of the tasks for which we now use the Net. Buying rail tickets, checking show times, posting personal ads, chatting, and searching for phone numbers were all made remarkably easy. Obviously, the bureaucratic France Telecom, a government agency, presaged a lot of Net entrepreneurs. Although a closed network limited a great many benefits of this early version of the Internet, it also kept some bad things at bay, like viruses.

Because the point of human interaction was simply a terminal, Minitel was fairly inexpensive to manufacture. As an effort to cut printing costs for phone books, these units were distributed free of charge, one per household, by request. That smart move quickly established the huge network of millions of users that was key to Minitel's success.

Quite a few different models of the terminal were made; this one is by Alcatel. The keyboard flipped up neatly to make a box that could sit smartly in a living room, and the design was pleasantly tactile. Not surprisingly, many assert that the existence of Minitel slowed French adoption of the Internet, and others make the opposite claim. The network is still operational—if a little less lively than in its prime—and Internet users can download an emulator that connects to the Minitel network whether they're in Paris or Portland.

NAME	OSBORNE 1
YEAR CREATED	1981
CREATOR	OSBORNE COMPUTER CORPORATION
COST	$1,795
MEMORY	64K RAM
PROCESSOR	Z80
OPERATING SYSTEM	CP/M

From giant machines that took up whole floors and weighed several tons, to something consumers could reasonably lug around, the thirty years between the UNIVAC and the Osborne 1 shrank commercial computing's size to a level at which something interesting could begin to happen. Business users could do their work wherever they needed to be (within limits), and they could take that work to where it needed to be.

Drawing inspiration from work done at (where else?) Xerox PARC on the Xerox Notetaker by Alan Kay—as well as on strong expertise gained from his careers as a technical writer and computer-book publisher—Adam Osborne, in conjunction with the circuit-board designer Lee Felsenstein, created a remarkable package. The Osborne 1 was a twenty-four-pound portable computer that set the standard for on-the-go business computers and affected the ways in which many personal computers would later be sold. Although the tiny monitor was smaller than the disk drives, and it would be two years before Compaq would make an IBM-compatible personal computer, the Osborne 1 was compelling enough to prove its worth to its audience and to sell well.

Incompatibility with other computers was not a major issue, especially with Osborne's efforts to make sure that the computer was bundled with a suite of software that could handle the most frequent business tasks, including a word processor, database, spreadsheet, and BASIC programming. Bundling like this was contrary to industry standards at the time, and if it were bought separately, the software would cost more than the computer. Osborne's understanding of the end user led him to a clear vision of how computer makers should build convincing, useful packages.

Unfortunately for Osborne, his computer may have proven the concept too well. After a successful couple of years, the Osborne 1 was eclipsed by competitors. The company was also hobbled by the early announcement of the Osborne II, while thousands of the original were still unsold. By 1983 the company was bankrupt.

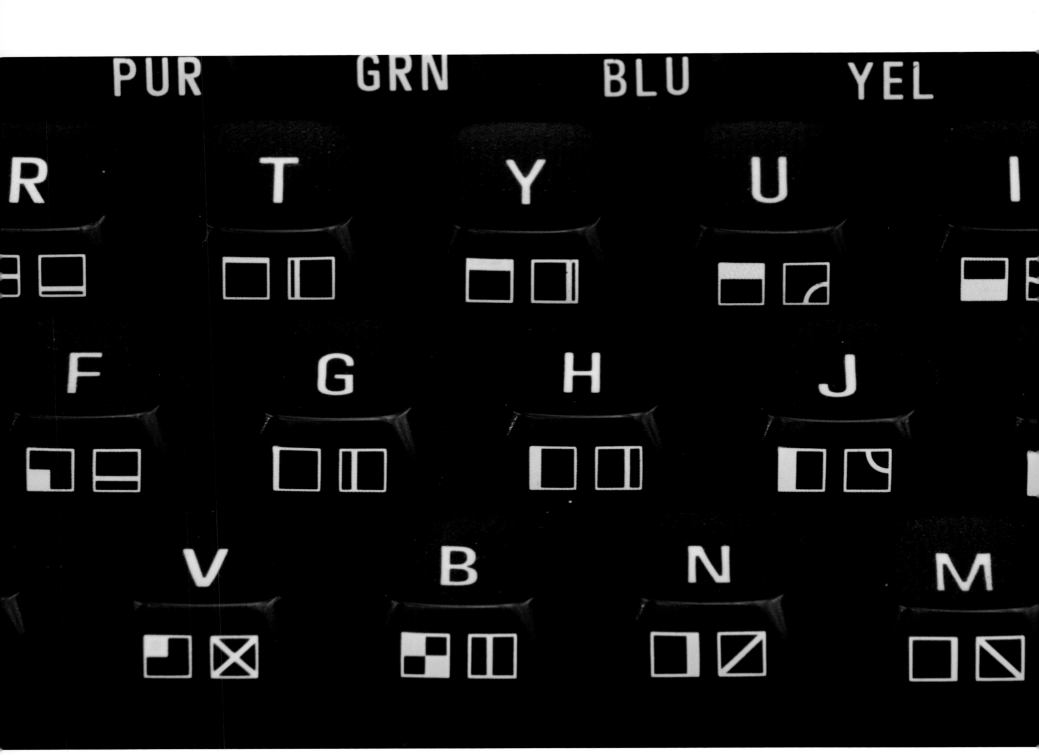

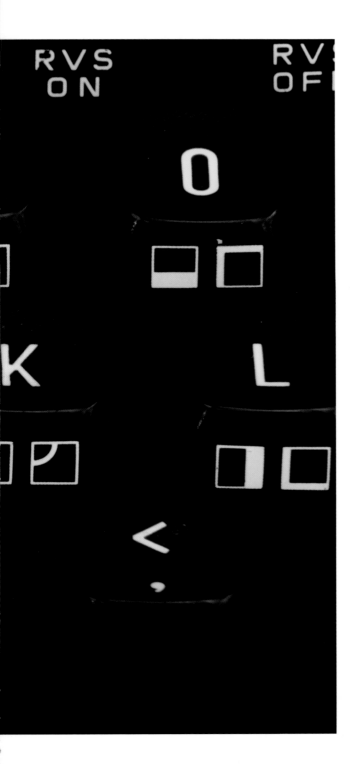

NAME	**COMMODORE 64**
YEAR CREATED	1982
CREATOR	COMMODORE
COST	$599
MEMORY	64K RAM
PROCESSOR	MOS TECHNOLOGY 6510

..//

One of the hallmarks of a great computer is its ability to launch subcultures. By that measure (among others), the Commodore 64 is in league with the greats. Of course, since somewhere in the neighborhood of twenty million units were sold in the 64's very long life span (1982 to 1993), it should come as no surprise that so many users would have a soft spot for their old computer. What is especially impressive is the clear example of how putting advanced sound and graphics capabilities into the hands of ordinary people could give rise to such a burst of creativity.

Named after the 64KB of RAM it boasted, the Commodore 64 was also a marketing success, and its sales in department stores and toy shops presaged the era when the video-games industry would be nipping at Hollywood's heels. In fact, this Commodore was first designed as a game console, but Commodore launched it as a full personal computer to keep its foot in the PC business as its VIC-20 aged. The switch worked, and Commodore harnessed lessons learned in interface design—such as the unique multifunction keyboard pictured here—and manufacturing to get a leg up on the competition.

Because it was an inexpensive computer with good memory and very strong graphics and sound capabilities, the 64 gave rise to what became known as "the demoscene," groups of young users demonstrating their programming prowess by crafting introductory screens that were often flashed as a kind of opening-credits sequence for hacked software. Many of these young scenesters went on to careers in the world of computer gaming and graphics.

COMMODORE 64, 1982

COMPAQ PORTABLE

NAME	**COMPAQ PORTABLE**
YEAR CREATED	1983
CREATOR	COMPAQ COMPUTER CORPORATION
COST	$3,590
MEMORY	128KB RAM
PRCOSSOR	INTEL 8088
OPERATING SYSTEM	MS-DOS

..//

Like the Osborne 1, the Compaq Portable drew from the design of the Xerox Notetaker, featuring a protective flip-down screen that doubled as a keyboard. What made Compaq's slightly heavier unit stand out was that it was 100 percent IBM PC—compatible. This remarkable "cloning" was made possible by teams of programmers who reverse-engineered IBM's BIOS (Basic Input/Output System). While the IBM PC used freely available parts and MS-DOS (and Microsoft was ready to sell that to anyone), the proprietary IBM BIOS was copyrighted.

Setting out to copy the IBM PC, Compaq approached making the clone as a combination engineering and legal challenge. One team analyzed the BIOS and then described to the second team (which had no contact with the BIOS) how the new system would function. The million-dollar effort worked, and the era of the IBM clone—powered by a Microsoft operating system and an Intel processor—had begun. Soon, aside from those made by Apple, nearly any personal computer would be an IBM clone, and the acronym PC came to stand for this new standard.

This interoperability had some advantages, such as reducing the need for a software bundle like the one included with the Osborne 1, as economies of scale brought down the cost of software—sometimes to nothing.

NAME	# MACINTOSH
YEAR CREATED	1984
CREATOR	APPLE COMPUTER, INC.
COST	$2,495
MEMORY	128KB SEMICONDUCTOR
PROCESSOR	MOTOROLA 6800
OPERATING SYSTEM	MAC SYSTEM SOFTWARE OS 1.0

..//

A famously Orwellian Super Bowl commercial announced the Macintosh to the world and did its best to cement earlier perceptions of Apple as an innovator and mark the brand forever as a tool in the great fight against conformity and for creative freedom. Like many home systems, the Macintosh was a neat package: a self-contained beige box housed the CPU, monochrome screen, and floppy-disk drive, and a keyboard and mouse were the appendages that allowed interaction. The mouse, particularly, in combination with the Graphical User Interface, or GUI, was a way of manipulating data that made sense on both visual and physical levels: clearly it drew something from light pens, but with some distance and abstraction from the screen that lent it more power.

Many of the Mac's innovations were famously inspired by the work of researchers at Xerox PARC, but it was Steve Jobs and his team of young engineers who were able to envision where these innovations were headed, and to run with them all the way to the market. Sure, the Mac made use of technologies that had been invented elsewhere, but putting them together in a package that was successfully built and marketed was, if not as quickly and literally liberating as the TV commercial promised, certainly a huge leap forward in the interface between humans and computers.

A step back was the abandonment of color. With the achromatic early Macs, Apple turned its back on what had helped set the Apple II apart. The Mac also lacked a hard drive, which made it completely dependent on the small-capacity floppy drive, and it had no fan, which caused hardware failures for many users. But the friendly little box made up for that with a smiley welcome screen and cute icons that personalized the user's experience. Not surprisingly, some people branded it a toy. But for those who saw the compelling, easy-to-use interface as a mark of sophistication rather than of childishness, the Mac became indispensable—it just took a few iterations until the value of the system could blossom.

NAME	**GOOGLE FIRST PRODUCTION SERVER**
YEAR CREATED	1996
CREATORS	GOOGLE, INC.
COST	$3,590
MEMORY	128K RAM
PROCESSOR	INTEL 8088
OPERATING SYSTEM	MS-DOS

../ //

With the rise of Internet ubiquity and the sudden critical mass of information unleashed by the World Wide Web, the necessity for search engines that worked well became critical. And just as early search engines were settling in, two students from Stanford had the idea for an engine that ranked a match not only by how closely a particular Web page matched someone's search words, but also by how many other sites were linked to the page. Adding that measure to each search created an index of reliability, or what might be called "social standing," that boosted the number of users of Google.com, which quickly became the most popular search engine on the Web, besting competitors such as HotBot and AltaVista.

Using a similarly clean, algorithmically-based method of serving up advertisements to people who searched according to a product or company's search terms quickly boosted Google's revenue, and after an iconoclastic IPO that did terrifically well, Google quickly became one of Silicon Valley's most successful companies, bringing in more than six billion dollars in 2005.

The power of the network is something that actually drives Google's own technology. Using inexpensive PCs wired together to form a network allowed Google to harness the power of large-scale computing at a cheaper price than would otherwise have been the case. Shown here is one of about thirty racks that constituted the initial Google server farm. Keeping track of failures in a system like that is important, and the Google search system allowed for server failure and routed around it.

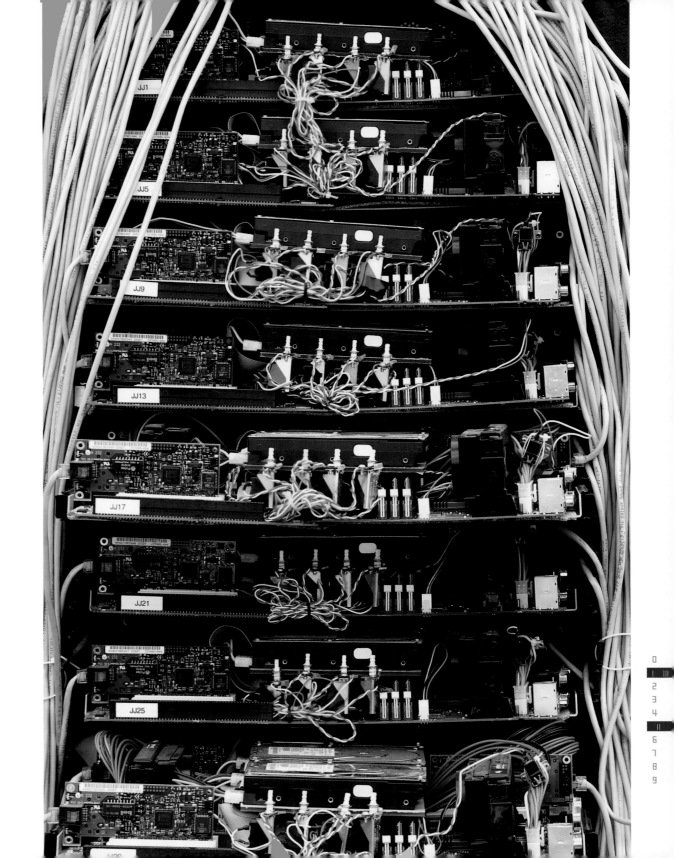

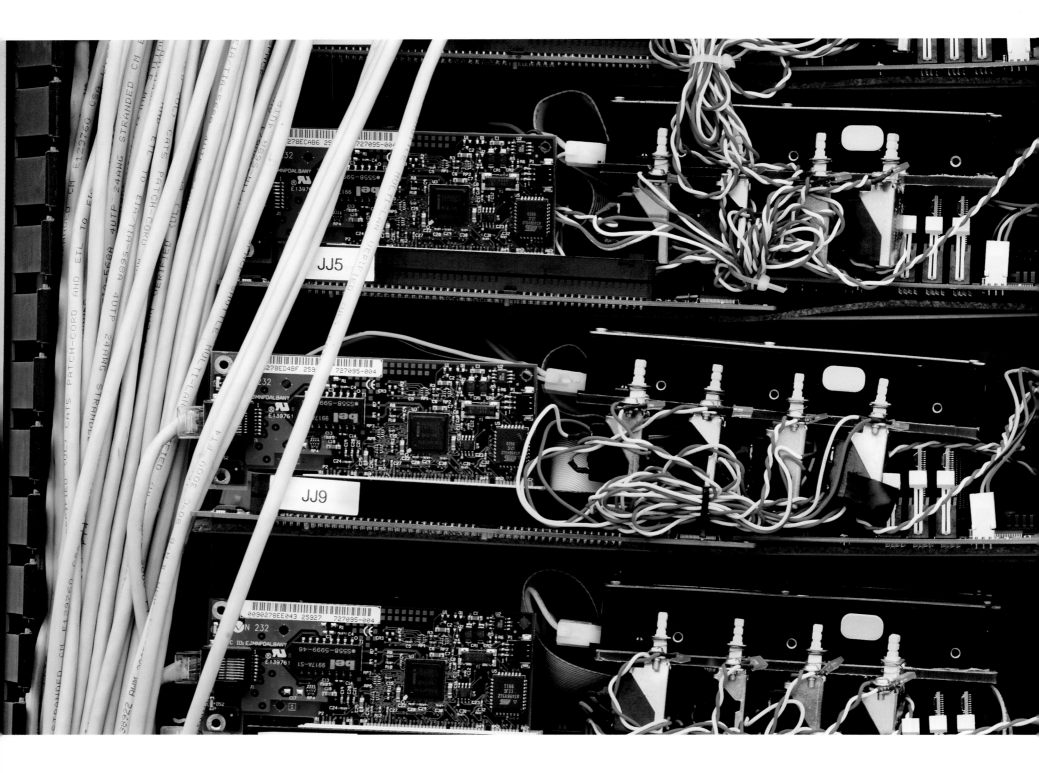

GOOGLE FIRST
PRODUCTION SERVER, 1996

ACKNOWLEDGMENTS / BIBLIOGRAPHY

..//

I wish to thank my wife, Dawn, for her love and support and just listening to me. My children, Nicole and Nicholas, for teaching me and supporting me. My two best friends, Eric Gray and Timothy Archibald, for listening way too much. My coauthor, John Alderman. My editors at Chronicle Books, Alan Rapp and Bridget Watson Payne. My agent, Deborah Ayerst. My brothers and sister, Chris, Tom, and Jody. My father-in-law, Dominic Fuclie, for teaching me. My father and mother for having me. Everyone at the Computer History Museum that has helped me—John C. Toole, Steven Brewster, Kirsten Tashev, Karen M. Tucker, Chris Garcia, and everyone else. Joe Matulich and Peter Menzel, special thanks for helping me get started. All my friends who have listened to me—Richard Morgansteen, Brian Smith, Amy Sherburne, Carol Halebain, Ed Caldwell, Thomas Broening, Stephanie Rausser, Jonathan Saunders, Eric Millette, Martha Bardach, Olivier Laude, Brian Smale, Bob Sacha, Mia Foster, Cindy Charles, Robert Holmgren, Sinead Duffy, Leslie Borden, Elizabeth Ely and Nikolaevich. Everyone who has helped me along in this life that I did not mention.   MARK RICHARDS

I'd like to thank Alan Rapp and Bridget Watson Payne from Chronicle Books for their patience and help; Mark Richards, for his amazing images; Dag Spicer, John Toole, Karen Tucker, and Kirsten Tashev from the Computer History Museum for inspiration; Garrick Schmitt and Marisa Gallagher from Avenue A | Razorfish for indulgence; Peter McGuigan for advice; David Pescovitz for wisdom; Ernest Alderman for the TRS-80 and Macintosh; and Wanida Wannapira for 24-hour support and loveliness.   JOHN ALDERMAN

MUCH OF THE RESEARCH FOR THIS BOOK WAS PROVIDED IN DOCUMENTATION BY AND CONVERSATIONS WITH THE STAFF OF THE COMPUTER HISTORY MUSEUM. THE FOLLOWING SOURCES PROVIDED ADDITIONAL INFORMATION ON THESE MACHINES.

CAMPBELL-KELLY, MARTIN, AND WILLIAM ASPRAY. *Computer: A History of the Information Machine.* New York: Basic Books,1999.

CERRUZI, PAUL E. *A History of Modern Computing.* Cambridge: MIT Press, 1998.

FREIBERGER, PAUL, AND MICHAEL SWAINE. *Fire in the Valley: The Making of the Personal Computer.* 2d ed. New York: McGraw-Hill, 2000.

LAING, GORDON. *Digital Retro: The Evolution and Design of the Personal Computer.* Cambridge: Ilex, 2004.

PESCOVITZ, DAVID. "Modern Art." *Wired* 7.11 (1999).

THE FOLLOWING WEB SITES ALSO PROVIDE HELPFUL ASSISTANCE WITH ANY FURTHER READING.

http://ftp.arl.mil/~mike/comphist/eniac-story.html
http://www.atariarchives.org/bcc3/showpage.php?page=290
http://channel9.msdn.com/Showpost.aspx?postid=123333
http://www.computerhistory.org/
http://www.computerworld.com/printthis/2006/0,4814,108568,00.html
http://www.rgshoup.com/prof/SuperPaint/
http://www.trs-80.com/
http://video.google.com/videoplay?docid=-7426343190324622223
http://www.woz.org/letters/general/94.html
and, of course, wikipedia.com.

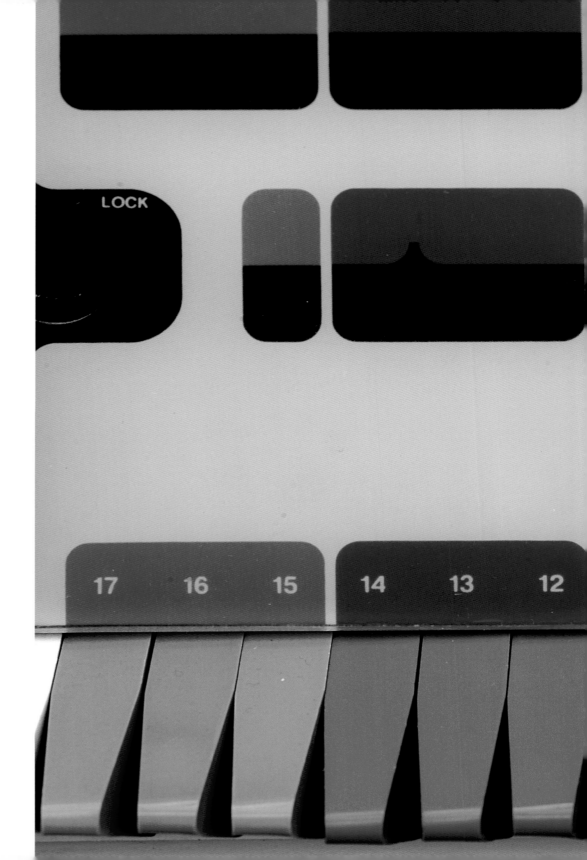

INDEX

..//

INDEX

..//

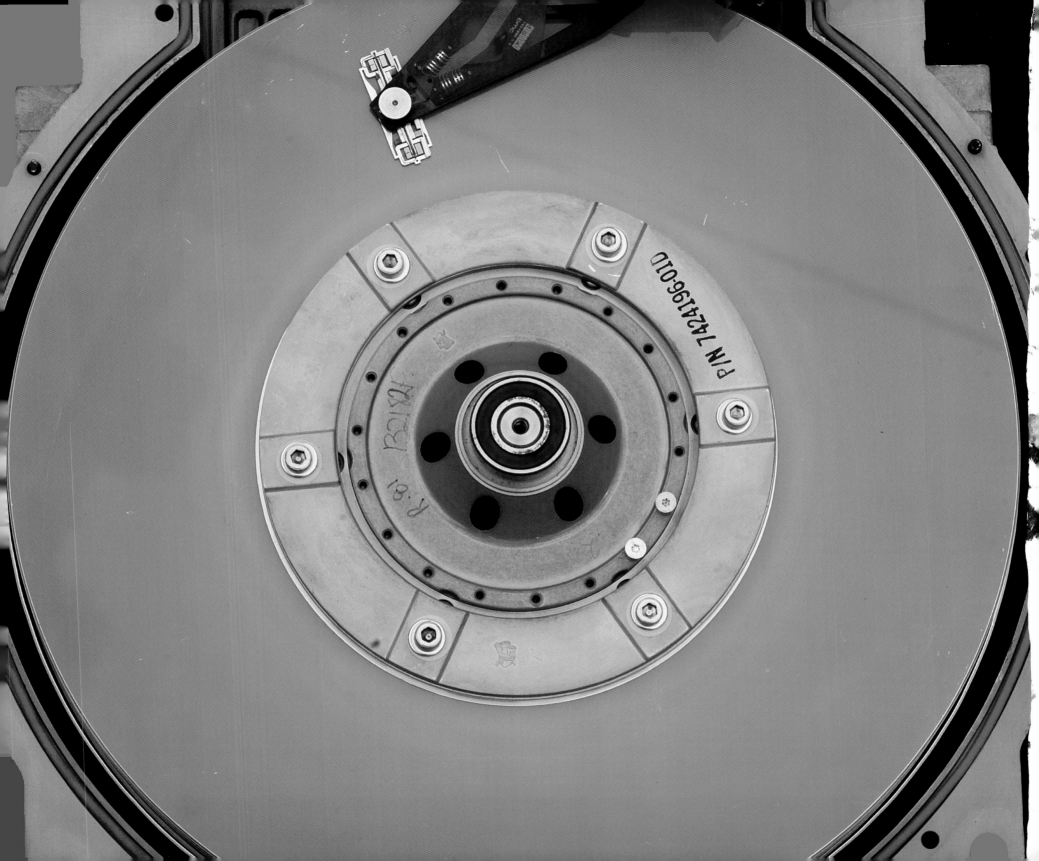